Last

House

Also by M. F. K. Fisher

M.F.K. Fisher

 Last

House

Reflections, Dreams, and Observations

1943–1991

Pantheon Books   New York

The following selections have been previously published:
Napa Valley Tables: The Folio of Food & Wine: "The Best Meal
I Ever Ate" (Spring 1990). • *The New York Times Magazine:*
"Journeys" appeared as "The Way It Was, and Is"
(October 7, 1984). • "My Grown-Up Ears" was originally
published in *Living Philosophies* (Doubleday, 1990).

Judith Clancy's drawing, on page 2, copyrighted by and used with
the permission of the estate of Judith Clancy.

Library of Congress Cataloging-in-Publication Data

Fisher, M. F. K. (Mary Frances Kennedy), 1908-1992
Last house: reflections, dreams, and observations, 1943-1991 /
M. F. K. Fisher.
p.   cm.
ISBN: 0-679-77411-4
1. Fisher, M. F. K. (Mary Frances Kennedy), 1908-1992—Biography.
2. Authors, American—20th century—Biography.
3. Food writers—United States—Biography. I. Title.
PS3511.I7428Z466   1995
641'.092—dc20   94-40948   [B]

Book design by Cheryl Cipriani

Printed in the United States of America
Random House Web Address: http://www.randomhouse.com/
First Paperback Edition, 1997

2 4 6 8 9 7 5 3 1

Contents

Introduction

NORAH BARR, MARSHA MORAN,
PATRICK MORAN

*L*ast House is M. F. K. Fisher's last book. It spans five decades and is her final word, in her own hand, in her own voice.

It is also the one book—out of more than twenty-five, written over her lifetime—that was literally the most difficult for her to write. *Last House* began in the early 1980s as Mary Frances's "secret project" and ended just prior to her death in June of 1992 as her final undertaking. Along the way, its form and content changed dramatically, and what started out as a collection of random thoughts, ideas, and digressions metamorphosed into a more serious and sometimes painful personal account of the aging process.

Mary Frances first envisioned *Last House* as an anthology of eclectic information that Fisher readers might at one time or another find useful, or at the very least interesting. She originally saw the book as a literary glory hole, brimming with promise, potential, and an occasional surprise or two. She thought then that the project might take the form of an alphabet, which could contain the observations of a writer who with age could strip away layers of pretense. She began work on the manuscript soon after she moved into Last House on the Bouverie Audubon Preserve in Glen Ellen, California.

From the outset Mary Frances was filled with ideas and enthusiasm. Indeed, her working folders are stuffed with small pieces of paper on which just a word or two serve as seeds for future germination and illumination. Unfortunately, however, she had neither the time nor the energy to expand on many of these thoughts, for soon after commencing work on *Last House,* Mary Frances began to be overwhelmed by a combination of physical limitations, and the struggle to put words to paper grew progressively more difficult. First came arthritis and then Parkinson's disease, both of which in their own cheerless ways deprived Mary Frances of the mechanical ability to transfer her thoughts directly to print. And although neither illness diminished her ability to formulate thoughts, what had once been a short sashay from imagination to page at nineteen—or thirty-two or even sixty-five—became at eighty a truly formidable crossing.

Arthritis made typing impossible. And the Parkinson's cramped her handwriting into tortured contours whose jagged outlines only one or two people were able to decipher. Yet despite these unwelcome twin sisters of old age, Mary Frances's work continued to flourish. For still there was her voice—breathy and thin and curiously adolescent—which matched a style that had always been natural, conversational, accessible; thus dictation was something that came easily to her, and some of the material in *Last House* was created in this manner. In the late 1980s, Mary Frances, hoping to embrace technology to her advantage, took a turn at using a tape recorder to compose her works, and a number of pieces were produced first on tape, transcribed, and then edited by her own hand.

Finally, the Parkinson's stole Mary Frances's voice, although it was apparent that the disease had done nothing to diminish her ability to think or her determination to tell others what was on her mind. When it became increasingly obvious that she would be unable to finish *Last House* as she had first conceived the book, Mary Frances decided to include a number of previously written, unpublished pieces. Yet even this was a painstaking process since she could no longer read and had to depend on others to be her eyes. The sorting of material appropriate to *Last House* required numerous readings of earlier works that had been accumulating in cartons at the far end of her bedroom. It took many months, and it was very near the time of her death when these pieces were finally added to the work that Mary Frances had previously done on *Last House.* By then, the writings that seemed to fit the book, and those that Mary Frances was drawn to, were quiet, sober, and often about aging, and even death and dying. The memory with which she chose to begin the book was written when Mary Frances was young, vigorous, and in love. It is a dreadful picture of the lives of young men in World War II drained through the Golden Gate. The book ends with a reminiscence about, and a longing for, a few beloved friends and pets that had died many years earlier.

Throughout the 1980s, Mary Frances recorded her long night thoughts, as she worked, became famous against her will, and was dealt the sharp blows of catastrophic illness that led to her death. She was honest and brave, and had to be honest, brave, and witty as well, for a much longer period of time than she would have wished. Everyone alive wonders how they will die, and how they will face death when it happens. Most of us are quite practiced at denial, but we welcome a book that gives us a few hints about how it can be done, by an honest writer, with superb grace.

For those fortunate enough to have witnessed or participated in Mary Frances's struggle to continue working during this period, there can be no greater source of inspiration, nor additional need of confirmation that the process of creation—for a writer or for anyone else—is as necessary as breathing, and critical in sustaining one's dignity and humanity. And although senescence forms the backdrop for many of the later pieces in *Last House,* this in not in the end the work of someone whose powers are in decline. Rather, it is an affirmation of the wisdom of taking on life—and death— as one's only real work.

Last

House

Why Again

At first, in the immediate impact of grief,
The body lay criss-cross.
The arms were spread out, and the legs stretched.
Gradually the immediate impact of grief grew less.
The legs came up, and crossed at ankles.
Arms folded softly across the wracked chest cage,
And the abandoned heart softened and came alive again.
The body grew quiescent, receptive,
A chrysalis, not dead
But reviving, curling into a further acceptance of the same
    process, the same physical position.

Within, there was still protest.
Why again, asked the vigorous spirit.
This time is surely enough, to be stretched out and pinned,
Pickled in the brine of the spirit.

No, said the spirit.
But the legs straightened and then pulled up,
The wracked arms crossed with gentle resignation over the
    breasts,
And the life began to slow to the waiting throb in the ever-
    hollowed still soft bosom.

Everything was ready for more.

—*St. Helena, California, 1965*

1
War

She . . . is it I? Is it the woman I once knew? Is it a stranger walking in my shoes, accustoming herself to the unusual phases of this life? . . . she went down the stairs unwillingly. The house was new to her, and she had crept first up to the second story to snitch the flashlight from the table by Elsa's bed. It was late. Elsa breathed heavily, luxuriously. The woman . . . yes, it is, or was, I . . . breathed heavily too, from all the stairs that she had climbed to get inside the door of this San Francisco house she was renting for herself and her baby and Elsa, who shared the care of the child. She stood listening to the easy breathing, in, out, in, of Elsa. Then with the flashlight she went down to the first floor of the house, and on down into the strange mossy bowels, to where the furnace hummed and whuddered. It lay, strange to her eyes, in a little room of extra-fancy bricks, like a monster in a special cage. The bricks seemed to hum with it. The lights quaked. She touched the bricks, and then the button on the nearest light, and when for a minute it went out and she felt the hot brick under her hand, she was blown into a trillion inescapable atoms. Then she thought of the little child upstairs, and Elsa breathing with such trust into the foggy air. She withdrew, both from the brick and from the surcease of fantasia. The air about her shook, and she was downtown, downtown in an office, laughing into the sardonic laughter of a man who said bitterly, "There is nothing left. Why do we bother to dine anywhere?" "Do you mean we should stay here and drink sherry?" she asked with a kind of tentative irony, or at least so she thought. "No," he said, and looked sharply at her, and out of the window she looked at the side of the Wells Fargo Building and thought in one wordless rush of express coaches and prairies and Lola Montez and even of a bar at the Palace Hotel where pictures of Mark Twain and Lola and old photographs in fake gold frames hang tidily above a lot of drunken heads. She looked again, and the air was sharp, and simply because it was over the bay and she knew it was over the bay, she thought of it as sharp and cold. "No," she said, "I didn't mean that either. We should go to a bar." They went to several, and everywhere there were two kinds of men and one kind of woman. As the evening went on they became more conscious of this fact. They commented on it, and through the good honest California wine and the fairly honest California brandy, they commented on it. They commented on it at the Fair, which was a pub where the bartender was old and made them a Gibson with loving care. Then they commented on it at Ernie's, or at least that was probably the name of the place, where when the man asked for a plain Dutch gin for her and a Gibson for him, the bartender said violently, "Oh, for God's sake, let's mix it in one shaker! What difference does it make?" Then when the man said with a kind of muted, old-school astonishment, "But the lady wants a straight gin," the bartender got a crumpled look on his face and became embarrassingly humble and even cringed, and the lady could hardly swallow the straight gin. (I was the lady, at least there.) And then they commented again on the two kinds of men and the one kind of woman in the bar at the Palace where a mural of Mark Twain hangs over the bottles, and all around the room are quaintly framed prints of his period and people under them on sofas who should be framed and perhaps are. The bartender was young there. He knew the lingo of soldiers, although most of the men he served were lieutenant commanders and, once or twice each evening, an admiral. When the man and woman (yes, I! I!) came in, he made them a passable Gibson, and almost at once they began talking about how hard it was to grow old and have no place to go but alone or in company to such an upper-class bar, and how sad it was to be old without philosophy, and a very young officer of the navy said, "Will you please excuse me if I butt in?" He had a bourbon and water in one hand, and there were dark tan circles above his cheekbones, and his eyes were young. "Of course not at all certainly," the man and woman said. "I heard what you said. It is absolutely right. The attitude . . . What is there, after all . . . What right have people . . . I mean . . ." The young officer waved his glass, and his tired innocent eyes looked worriedly at the two people. They felt as old as all the hills of Israel. Pretty soon they got off their high seats and left him standing there, and although they had been more than nice and he had been equally discreet, they worried for some time about whether they should have invited him to dine with them. He had been drinking bourbon. They were going to drink a Château de Camensac, 1923. How could they? They felt guilty, foolish, stupid . . . and yet the bottle waited for them. It had been waiting since 1923, or at least such reasoning seemed logical. And there the bottle sat on the table, waiting to be violated, in the candlelight, in the soft music that flowed over all the medals and all the taut mouths and the thirsty eyes. And it was good wine. The food was less good. The maître d'hôtel came up and whispered sadistically that the chef had sacrificed his one free afternoon to drive into the country for the meat. There was no butter. The flavors were strained. But it was well served, all of it, and the wine, tired as an old man with blue veins on his hands, lifted them into a special paradise. They sat like humans full of opium, and watched the people float weakly, obliviously, past them. There was one strong-faced woman who ordered a horrible mess of precooked wartime food, and ate it heartily and then smoked a long thin cigarette without touching it, as if it were a rare cigar. And there were tables everywhere of soldiers and sailors, all of them hungry for their loves or for unknown loveliness, who ate doggedly at expensive nothings, or perhaps ordered steak-and-kidney pie and waited for it and then pushed it away. One man leaned heavily against the shoulder of a pinch-faced supercilious corporal and told him of his dead son, and the corporal, who had perhaps looked down on that son's grave, listened almost mockingly and, if he had not been a brave fairy, would have pushed the old man in the face. He hated the old man. He hated himself. And there were other things to hate too. There were the two kinds of men and the one kind of woman. After the winey meal, in a bar up the hill in the Italian part of the city, the man and woman felt it. The woman, because of her fairly clear-tracked past, dreaded to see two gently silly humans still called men come into a bar and lean gracefully against its edge, and then watch hackles rise on other humans in uniform. That happened, in and out, up and down, in the mirror in front of her, behind her. And women in fluffy fur coats rubbed themselves against the sailors to their left, rather than against the old heavy-lidded husbands to their right. And the soldiers and sailors brought in their friends. All the women seemed alike, so thirsty in this port, wanting to drink deep of the blood of life. And all the men were so desirous of being drunk, drunk up, made alive once before the great debauch of battle. The Golden Gate waited. It was a throat. It was a vein. Men flowed through it. It was a thirsty hole, and the bright blood of the world gushed in spurting convoys toward the East, every day, in the gray ugly ships fat with men. The men reasoned or they did not reason, but the women had but one course. And the woman who watched all that, the night of the bottle of Camensac 1923, thought that perhaps she had found the answer. Then she drank, after one or two brandies at La Tosca, an Americano, a sage biting mild drink. She looked down the bar at all the thirsty people. There were two soldiers getting ready either to beat up two dainty civilians next to them or go to sleep. There were a few pretty girls, from thirteen to sixty, and at the end of the bar, just beyond the espresso machine, was the star of a nearby floor show, complete with long eyelashes and cheaters and a boyfriend. In the air, over the sound of Nino Martini on the jukebox, she heard the foghorns blowing, and she thought of all the men waiting below-decks and of all the dog tags dangling on the warm-skinned ribs. Soon after that, at home, she went down into the strange cellar, full of the thoughts of love, and of the men everywhere who had no such warmth. She was full of pity. The furnace was humming. She opened the door, so staunchly lined with bricks. The round box glowed and with a startling suddenness roared and shivered. The dog tags came in a leisurely way into her mind, and then she thought of her child on the top floor of the tall wooden house, and then as all the whiteness wrapped around her, she saw the Golden Gate like an artery, a cut artery, with all the proud bitter men flowing out through it toward the East, in a rush, a gush, a stream, a hot flood that made her smile once more.

—San Francisco, California, 1943

2

Rex—I

There is a book I must write, and one I have long thought upon. Let me say that it will be about all good old people, of which I hope one day to be one; it is, perforce, about many I have known and lived with; it is about an oldster I would like one day to resemble. It is about Rex.

I shall draw upon my files I have kept for about twenty years, to put it safely, for long before then I was keenly conscious and even knowledgeable of the ways of old people. I thought, even so long back, that they must be even more important than I, and this, from a human being of fifteen or twenty years, is an almost monumental thought. Very soon after that I began to clip little sayings, quips, or bright quotations about the far from happy thoughts of people over sixty-five or seventy. (I do not rightly know when old age begins, but according to the welfare agencies and the insurance companies, two fairly respected authorities, it is at about such ages.)

I have kept my files going, to my intimates' amazement. I have countless clippings. I am glad. I can look, more or less at will, at what a baker's dozen of experts say about the physiological, emotional, glandular, gastronomical, gonadal-or-do-I-mean-glandular-again, psychological trends (if not traits) of those of us who are past fifty. It is a very reassuring picture.

I like old people.

I like to be old.

I'll write of Rex.

I have always known I would, but I've thought of it as past his coffin, over the hump of his disintegration, and in words tinged, imbued, weighted with the essences of my sorrow for a man lost to me.

Now I feel that I am strong enough, since he is, to write of him as an old man while he still is one.

Instead of waiting until he has died, and until my own harried emotions have settled into a kind of quiescent awe, I am, suddenly and unexpectedly, ready to write about him now, while he is alive, breathing, coughing, eating, defecating.

The best thing about this almost extrasensory decision is that I know it would meet with his approval if I cared to bother him about it. He acknowledges my small professional skills. He bows to my discretion. He would listen to my plan and smile with only slight apprehension, inevitable in a small-town editor, and then would read each chapter with a kind of patience impossible to anyone younger, fresher, less tolerant—anyone my age, for instance, forty-two instead of seventy-three.

That is why I think I should write the book about old age, about Rex, now, not later. It is the very fact that he does not much care, that he trusts me, that makes me want to put all these things into words—the things I have thought over a long time about old people and now *know* about such a fine, such an old, MAN.

I went in after he had turned his lights off and put the glasses beside his bed, and his face turned up to me like a child's when I leaned to kiss him. My heart turned over.

—*Whittier, California, 1950*

3

Rex—II

Hatred, hatred. What venom it distills. Tonight, filled with it, I give off poisonous exudations, I well know. Rubbing his feet, I could feel my hatred flow like bile through my fingertips into his strangely warm knobby venous toes ankles calves. Now, warm and alone in my bed, wrapped in a garnet shawl, sipping at an unwanted highball which I down almost as a punishment, I can smell the hated sourness on my hands, and can realize my puny foolishness to be so wretched, so voluptuously wretched.

My mind races volubly. Every word it says can lead in many a direction, and it is hard, as well as basically destructive, to force myself to follow one line of thought, or of suggestion.

God, but I have been angry tonight. By now I am coming into focus again. And even when I was most filled with the poison I knew my basic impotence, for I see no reason, really, for wounding Rex, no matter how slightly. He is old. He is tired. He is an astonishingly spoiled man: that is the crux of it, and I am too old and he is even too much older for me to try to show him how he could be easier to live with. Besides, I am not in love with him. Mother, and later Sis, tried hard to make him toe the lines they drew. They had rows. They wept. They stormed and sulked. As far as I can see he did not really ever hear them. But it was worth it, I suppose, because of the love. Me, I don't love him.

Now and then I loathe him, for the stupid waste, the basically timid arrogance in him. Mostly I accept him as a kind of fore-shadow of myself, for we are much alike, glandularly and in the basic timidity and the arrogance. (But I think I am wiser, and therefore less impregnable.) There are times, like tonight, quite possibly dictated by the tides, when I am filled with a consummate revulsion. Most of the time I shed off things that other women squirm at openly or must turn away from: the dribbles of urine on the floor by the toilet, the long sensual belches at breakfast, the knowledge that he is restrained and charmingly gallant for any goddamned fluffy fool of a scheming small-town Bovary. But now and then I cannot, or do not, shed my deep and perhaps instinctive distaste for my intimacy with my father. All his odors repel me, and at his age and with his background of cautious midwestern plumbing, his odors are many. (I know about the difficulties of keeping clean in the aged. I know about earlier conditioning. I know . . . Still I hold my breath when I must step over the steamy underwear on the sitting room floor at night in order to reach the toilet; and I hold my breath again when after the fairly neutralizing oil I put on the alcohol and it pulls out from the blue-white feet a wave of bitter fumes; and I hold my breath now, an hour later, not to smell my hands, scrubbed, oiled, but still subtly stinking of those poor trusting rotten feet.)

Yes, the odors repel me, although I know they are largely involuntary. The sounds repel me, the long masturbatory belchings when he need not restrain himself—that is, when he is with the children and me. The equally long and voluptuous pickings at his nostrils, while he reads at night or even sits over his coffee: they repel me. And I am *agacée,* hurt, rebuffed, annoyed, everything like that, when he slams into his room, leaving all the doors open, and pees noisily. (Often when I rub his feet they are still damp with the urine he has dripped casually.)

Yes, many things about living with this old man exasperate me. Usually, given the situation and my increasing capacity for dispassion, I can sublimate my feelings fairly successfully. But now and then I cannot, and the thing I have the hardest time with *always,* no matter what the tides, is his spitting. I know he has to spit. I know what is wrong with him, I'm sure much better than he does himself. I know all that. But Jesus Christ in a handbasket, he need not be so thoughtless; so self-absorbed, so morbidly preoccupied. Or need he, given his seventy-four years of preoccupation and self-absorption? How can I ask, or blame?

All I know is that when I came home from getting the girls at school, and hurried into the kitchen to start organizing One More Meal, and saw a foamy blob of his spittle in the sink, I was as near physical revolt as I have been for several years. I thought I would vomit. And all the time I was thinking, This is a very *healthy* reaction, the best one yet—you are healthy now, much better. (I think I was right, too!) I had to go out, as soon as I had flushed the sink. I made myself a distastefully strong drink. I thought, This might even make you drunk. (But it did not.)

I was censorious and quietly horrid with the children, as my obviously easiest outlet. (They were patient with me, and now I think with a desperate resignation that I would to God I had the past hours back again, with those two budding beautiful little creatures.) I kept on sneering and blaspheming—no, that's not the right word—in my mind, and making chitchat and swallowing food and recognizing many of my familiar impulses toward escape.

I kept telling myself how much more "normal" my present revolt was—no remorse, no guilt, just a damned good physical reaction followed by reasonable and reasoning resentment. Now and then as I sat amicably chatting, I contemplated A Good Scene. But I'm no good at them, and anyway I do *not* think they are right for children.

So—I went upstairs, and drew some creature comfort from an enema, which did indeed expurgate some of my rage. I lay down with Anne. She caressed me forgivingly with her slender dirty hands and made me feel both foolish and happy. Mary snored calmly in the other bed, but I did not feel that in her heart she was either calm or dormant. Then I went grudgingly downstairs, where a good fire burned. I felt mean and hateful. Rex picked at his nose in his own corner. I lay down, got up, moved about listlessly. It's either a scene or get out, I said. I'm no good at scenes. So . . . I got out. He felt my hatred, I know.

He went early to bed. He opened his sitting room door and tapped the jamb twice, our signal, and I turned off the tropical fish and the lights and fixed the fire screen and went in. I held my breath, and rightly. I flushed the yellow water down the toilet, and pushed the rug over the splashes of urine on the floor. I saw the teeth in the glass bowl, with flecks of food rising slowing in the water. The radio blasted, and as always, that annoyed me, for Rex knows it hurts my ears and that he can turn it up after I've rubbed his feet, but he never does. Often two or three stations blare together—two tonight. I thought that he'd bathed yesterday, but already he smelled like Wednesday instead of only Monday. I felt his toenails, like pieces of savage carving. He must go soon to the podiatrist—I must call for an appointment, and see that he puts it in his book, and then remind him and remind him.

All the time I was trying not to breathe, and increasingly I thought about hatred, and the different ways it can be what it is, and I grew more certain that this revulsion of mine tonight was a very healthy normal one. I did not hit anyone, except my children, with what I hope was a glancing spiritual blow (I do not say that lightly). I did not kick or yell or weep, although I was for a time near the last. *I* felt like hell. I took an enema. Then I drank a highball by myself with an electric pad turned to Low on my belly, and a chilly east air blowing over me, and the children breathing, perhaps disappointed but with confidence, in the other room.

I feel sorry, yes. Tonight I could not really *look* at Rex, because I was so angry at him for spitting in the sink: I knew he would see my anger. Perhaps that would have been a good thing. But I do not love him that way, and am not able to have good rousing battles with him. So I hide my bile. I don't think it really hurts me at all—except that I am still clumsy enough to vent some of it on the two people I love best, my innocent children. I sometimes feel that they know more than I, and therefore are as forgiving as they seem to be. But through my pores, through my lips pressed desperately upon their chaste temples, am I teaching them hatred?

—*Whittier, California, 1951*

4

Tea with
Agamemnon

One day in the spring in California, two women sit talking in a eucalyptus grove. There is a mountain behind them, snowy still, and under them sweet alyssum blooms with a wild heavy smell of honey in the sun. A dog lies watching, waiting for crumbs of love and cookies, as the humans drink tea with their own brands of easiness. Fredrika is the older, with long bare legs and a band of turquoise silk tied optimistically around her wisps of white hair; Mary Frances, the other, is remote and teasing. Both of them are shy, the way old friends can be without premeditation. Fredrika says, in her soft voice with the strange sweet crack in it, "They are all I remember about Greece, really. My mother got the recipe from her cook when we lived in Athens. I was about five, and Agamemnon and I . . ." Her voice fades vaguely, and she holds out a plate of little round flat cakes so dreamily that they almost slide off. The dog watches them, his tail wagging. Mary Frances takes the plate and puts it on her knees, and when she bites into one of the cakes, she sees the dog looking at her sadly, intently.

Mary Frances: They are good, delicious. Are they really honey cakes, the kind the gods ate?

Fredrika: Probably. Nothing changes in Greece—nothing basic, that is. Agamemnon lived next door to me and was about my age. His last name was Schliemann. His father unearthed Troy, you know, and his mother was Greek. I suppose she was beautiful —all Greek women are, in my mind at least, although I can't remember anything about them actually except that my nurse wore a black woolen dress that scratched my face when she carried me upstairs. My mother told me later how to make the honey cakes. Agamemnon and I would eat them in the afternoons on the long marble porch of his house, with goat's milk. That is, we did until my father discovered what the goats lived on in Athens.

Fredrika pauses and laughs in her shy way, bending over to put half a cookie between the dog's polite soft lips. Mary Frances drinks slowly at her cup of tea, watching her friend, smelling the honey in the air, and tasting it on her tongue.

Fredrika: Father couldn't understand why his children weren't thriving on goat's milk. It sounded so *Attic!* and therefore perfect. And then he saw that practically the only food the city goats had was the flour paste they licked off the huge paper funeral notices that were stuck up every day on the walls. He was horrified. He made himself taste a little of our milk, and sure enough it was pure paste, or so he swore later. So after that we didn't drink anything but lemonade, as far as I remember. (She adds firmly, as if reassuring herself:) I *don't* remember *much,* of course.

Mary Frances: Oh, yes you do. Tell more. Go on. Do these cakes really taste the same?

Fredrika: Not quite. Hymettos honey, from the hills around

Athens, is sweeter, because of all the thyme blossoms the bees have there.

Mary Frances: It goes with the sweet alyssum, today. What else do you remember?

Fredrika frowns, a little impatient at her stubborn friend. She speaks slowly at first: Well . . . nothing about food, really. There were dry gullies, like the ones here in this country, but often they were like torrents, like floods of purple and rose and lavender, with anemones. The flowers were higher than my knees. And then . . . then at Easter there were big hens' eggs, blown out and painted with Christ Crucified, in beautiful colors. You exchanged them with people, and they were as light as feathers, but they didn't seem to break. My mother still had one or two, when I was growing up in Connecticut. And of course there were the paschal lambs, roasting everywhere.

Mary Frances: Well?

Fredrika: Well, there wasn't much meat in Greece, I suppose. I don't think people ate it often. But at Easter almost everybody had a lamb. You'd see the boys and men carrying them home, hung over their necks, bleating. My father said they were always killed very tenderly . . . part of a sacrifice. Then all the insides, *everything*—(She interrupts herself:) Once Father went up to the monastery on Mount Athos, pulled up in a basket. He was a man. Women couldn't get *near* the place. And as the guest of honor he was served the roasted eyes of the lamb. He ate them, too . . . but it never left his mind again . . . They don't throw away anything at all, you know, and when the lamb is dead, they put all the parts except the carcass on a long fresh skewer of pinewood, highly seasoned, laced together with strings of the cleaned guts. That's called . . . (Fredrika hesitates and then looks at once pleased and confused.) Now, how on earth do I remember that? I haven't even *thought* the word for years! It's *kokoretzi*. It smokes and cooks beside the carcass of the lamb. That's on another long fresh spit. I think there must be handfuls of thyme inside it, because I can smell that mixed with the heavy smoke of the fresh pine boughs. At Easter you smell that everywhere in Greece. Or did. (She closes her mouth bitterly, as if ashamed of speaking of food once eaten in a land so sorely tried.)

Mary Frances, quickly, teasingly, to divert her: I thought you'd forgotten everything!

Fredrika, weighing two halves of a honey cake in her thin, weed-stained fingers and then giving the larger piece to the dog Pinto: Nonsense. It's as clear as yesterday. I stood looking from my window, and it was black-dark, so I was naughty to be awake. We lived near the great field where the soldiers had maneuvers. There was a circle three deep of evzones around the roasting pits, turning and basting. They laughed a lot, and they were the handsomest men in the world, with their stiff white skirts shining in the firelight, and their teeth flashing. There was music too, although I don't know know whether it was flutes or bagpipes or what. And the smell of the hot lamb meat and the burning pine boughs is something I'll never forget. Nonsense . . . it's as clear as yesterday. (Fredrika pushes back a lock of hair, and sits up very straight.)

Mary Frances: What went with it?

Fredrika: Oh, a pilaf, of course. My mother's recipe was for one cup of rice, washed well and dried, browned in four tablespoonfuls of butter or olive oil. Then one cup of tomato puree and three cups of good meat stock are brought to a boil and poured in, and the lid is put on tightly until the rice is tender and has absorbed all the juice. No stirring. Then the pilaf is shaken, and a dry cloth is put tightly over the top of the pan and the lid is put on again for about ten minutes.

Mary Frances: Like a risotto, practically. Simpler. Don't the Greeks use garlic or onions?

Fredrika: I don't remember ... Yes, of course ... but with the pilaf, I think, chopped fresh thyme or dittany, tossed in at the last.

Mary Frances: Dittany ... it sounds like something from Ophelia's song.

Fredrika: It's a lovely herb. It grows wild on the hills, with tiny blue flowers. It used to be thought so powerful for healing that when stags were wounded they ate it and the arrows fell out of them. It was called *dictamnus* ... or (and Fredrika coughs apologetically) so Father said. College professors' children keep strange things in their heads. But I do know a little dittany is wonderful in green salads. We should grow more of it in America.

Mary Frances: I read of a Greek pilaf of chicken in Escoffier, the other day. Mutton fat was used for browning the meat, which was cut up, and then ... *here's* an onion! ... an onion was browned, chicken consommé was added, and a chopped pimiento and a handful of currants. It was served in a ring of pilaf.

Fredrika: Yes. That would be Greek ... and good.

Mary Frances: How about wine, though? I've heard people say they hated Greek wine.

Fredrika: I was a little young for it, even as a substitute for goat's milk. But of course it has a lot of resin taste to it. The Greeks like that. They still chew resin. It's a delicacy, and used to be reserved for the upper classes. It is supposed to sweeten the breath, cleanse the teeth, all that ... And everywhere in Greece is that piney smell ... even in the roasted meats. It's so clean ...

Mary Frances: And did you and your Aristophanes—

Fredrika: *Agamemnon* ... (She adds dreamily:) Agamemnon Schliemann ...

Mary Frances: Did you have anything besides these wonderful, delicious, funny little honey cakes?

Fredrika: There were lots of cakes made of very thin layers of pastry called phyllo, with pounded dates and almonds and so on in between, but they were too rich for us children. Once in a while our nurses would give us a spoonful of rose-leaf jam. It was the sweetest, most perfumed thing I've ever eaten. I loved it then, but when I've tasted it since in Near East restaurants, I've almost hated it. Once I tried to make it, but I think maybe the roses weren't red enough, or my heart had grown up too much. (Fredrika coughs self-consciously, as always when she feels she has said something less restrained than she was brought up to feel was ladylike.) I took equal parts of clean dry rose leaves, the darkest red in the garden, and sugar. I moistened the sugar with equal parts of lemon juice and water until it was easy to stir the petals, and then let the whole thing lie in the sun until it was hot and well melted. Then I boiled it for about a half hour, stirring it all the time. And then I didn't really like it.

Mary Frances: Did you ever eat the jelly made from cactus apples that is served with grilled wild birds in northern Mexico? That is very sweet and perfumed, too.

Fredrika: No. But it couldn't be worse than the rose-leaf jam I used to think was so delicious. Of course I was young . . .

Mary Frances: And in love . . .

Fredrika, standing up abruptly and lifting the tea tray: Well, I *did* like having tea with Agamemnon!

—*Hemet, California, 1951*

5

Eaters

She sat facing me, one table ahead and to my right, in the noisy pleasant place. Deft men in red jackets skimmed between us, and short thicker busboys carried loaded trays of used silverware and dishes. The place was a popular crowded famous old fish house, and people who went there, inevitably to wait for a table, did so because they liked it very much.

I wondered about the old woman whose face I was not precisely forced to watch, but which came often into my gaze.

She did not look relaxed and hungry and gay, like the rest of the chattering chewing talking people. They all leaned across the plain uncovered tables and ate as they talked, eagerly. She sat stiffly upright. Her eyes were always on the man across from her, or sliding across to me as if for criticism or comment. She ate with precise good manners.

There was behind her well-bred front a feeling of dismay, perhaps of desperation. I did not like her face, for it was drained and stiff, with pale blue eyes, a thin unhappy mouth, and flat white cheeks under a coy blue hat set on her carefully curled, short snow-white hair. She wore fashionable junk jewelry in her ears and around her stringy old neck, and her blue dress matched her hat in a coquettish way. She was what Philip Wylie would call a "Mom."

She was perhaps seventy. The man facing her and with his back to me, I at first assumed to be her own age. He sat upright exactly as she did, with hair almost as white and close-cropped above his stiff neck. He was perhaps twenty years younger, though, and he was most probably her son.

He wore a white collar and a dark coat cut in such a clerical style that at first I thought him to be a priest. When he stood up at the end of the sterile prim meal, I saw that his slacks were gray. As far as I could see, he never said more than a monosyllable to the old woman sitting across the little table from him. Some of the remarks she made were sour or complaining ones, judging from her tight mouth and the way she looked almost shamefacedly toward me. As she stood up to leave, she smiled at him, but it was a polite grimace taught her long ago, a kind of female thanks for the food she had eaten. Then she awkwardly put on her own coat and followed the son out through the crowded noisy tables.

He had read all during the meal, and as she stood, he too got up, put his book in his pocket, and walked out confidently, knowing she was behind him.

I stared a little, trying to see the titles of the books (or rather the paperbacks) he was reading so insolently in the face of her attempts to look like the rest of the people. They were reviews, perhaps, printed in two columns on limp paper, and he tucked two of them in his jacket pocket at the end of the meal. I suspected that they were either religious or pedagogical.

It is interesting that while I was really observant of what different kinds of men and women were ordering and eating, all around my table, I never once looked at what had been on the savage plates, the cold venomous platters, set before these two. There was a feeling of such scorn and despising and fear between the woman and the younger man that the thought of their breaking bread together was beyond me.

As the man stood up and the old woman across from him struggled into her carefully matching blue coat and put on her gloves, and as he slid his flat books with an accustomed gesture into his pocket, I noticed the straight thin line of his body. He was almost gaunt, and very consciously and austerely well tailored. I forget about his hands. But when he turned with a kind of insolence away from the woman, who still smiled a little, very politely, I had to avert my eyes from his face. Instead of matching the good set of his grayed head upon his straight thin neck, it was small but heavy and brutal in a pinched way obviously inherited from his mother. He looked infinitely self-indulgent in a very attenuated way, a hermit on a cozy pillar or flagpole. Sensual disdain was in every cell of his face, and in a flash I recognized the deft white sensitive fingers that could torture other bodies and his own, the quick tongue behind the thin lips, the skill and detestation of his secret life. The books in his pocket and the cold intelligence of his spoken clipped monosyllables were his disguise.

The old woman had shaped him. He believed himself free, except for having to sit opposite her in a crowded restaurant filled with the vulgar. He thought his outward rebellion and arrogance were his escape, but really she was stronger than he.

—*Berkeley, California, 1959*

6

Death of a Mouse

Before I try to start work again after several weeks of illness and convalescence, I think I should make some sort of report on the surprising attempt of my soul to reappear. Perhaps I should call this report "Notes Found in an Empty Achromycin Bottle," although the actual encounter with my soul for the second time, as well as my sudden ability to recall the first one, happened before I began taking the pills.

I knew for some time that I did not feel well, but I had no idea that I would become so defined by pain and fever that I could be near such an experience as the one I had. Four days and nights of the white tablets emptied the little bottle, and I was pronounced ready to begin to recover.

The recovery has been interesting and lengthy, and while it still goes on I feel impatient of the waste of time and of myself, and yet almost voluptuously, I cling to the need for sleep and miss the cosmic mouse that squeaked to me in my left lung when I was alone and wandering.

Now I am nearly well again, and must begin to stay upright and make the correct moves in the right directions, and not wonder too much about when my soul will come again.

Physical illness is ugly and I shall speak of it as little as possible, and only in connection with the other thing.

Apparently I was really ill, and like most stubborn healthy people I was incredulous about it, so that I waited several days before I admitted that I could not get up and make breakfast for my family, and then spent five days in bed before I started to cry when I confessed that I needed a doctor's help, no matter how pill laden and generally unwelcome.

The night before I made this last feverish pain-stiff admission, I coughed steadily in a small dry exhausting way, perhaps a little more so than for the previous long time. It seemed by then a normal way of existing. The poor body was at once all-absorbing in the energy it demanded but at the same time almost despicably unimportant, thanks to long fasting. I listened to the cough, always on the same level of sound and effort, with a detached recognition. Brother Cough, I said philosophically, as to a longtime companion. Friend Squeak, I said affectionately, for it was the mouse living in my dark hot lung-cabin with the rigid roof beams and the walls so tinder dry that comforted me with thin songs and chatter.

Then that night the speed and sound of the cough changed, and the mouse multiplied into mad rats eating me. And up into my throat moved my soul.

I got out of bed, as if to meet it courteously.

Dreadful sounds were coming from me.

The soul, smooth and about the size of a small truffle or scallop or a large marble, rose firmly into my upper throat. It cut off my wind, but that did not matter for the time we both needed.

I knew what it looked like, for I had seen it long ago. I knew its color and its contours and its taste, for I had held it in my hand once and studied it and then chewed and swallowed it to wait within me. But this was not the time for its return.

"Go back," I cried out to it, in language it recognized through the wild coughing, and through the way the bloody rats scrabbled behind it to escape with all of me dragging from their teeth, with my lungs my liver my guts all waiting torn and ready to stream out like flags behind them, if my soul should flee first, leaving only bones and shell and the little mouse.

"Go back," I begged ferociously as it stayed there for years that night, turning slightly as breath pushed it and the rats waited. It was interesting to feel it turn, for I remembered its shape, pure and smooth in my red gullet.

There was very little left now, of the breath it had trapped behind it with the rats, and indeed of me the fighter. It seemed as if most of my solar plexus had been torn loose by the impatient invaders. If the soul left me then, I feared fastidiously that I would seem to be vomiting, but it would be *me,* not some extraneous thing like fried fish wolfed in a greasy restaurant. It would be unworthy.

"*NO.* No, *wait,*" I begged it, and I promised to accept the next visit it would pay me, and I reminded it of our long years together.

I told it, in a flash as long as the eon of time it takes for one molecule to wed another, of our first meeting, and of the mystery and respect and indeed affection I had battened on from that day.

I was about five, maybe four. It was a beautiful morning, maybe spring or winter but good, maybe a Saturday. I lay in my bed waiting for my little sister to awaken, studying the white painted iron of the bedsteads. Surely there were birds talking, and curtains stirring in the windows of the pleasant room, and sounds from downstairs, but all I remember is that in a ruthless slow way, but without any pain or fear for me, my young small soul rose up into my throat and then came out.

I did not choke. I did not spit it out. It simply rose from inside me, glided along the root and the rest of my tongue, and then lay in the palm of my hand, which must have been waiting for it in front of my mouth. I was dazzled and yet unastounded.

It was about as big as a little hazelnut or chickpea, of the subtlest creamy white, like ivory but deeper. It was delicately convoluted, like the carvings on a human brain or a monkey's, but worn by thousands of years to its present silkiness without ever being in danger of turning into a ball or egg. It was perfection in form.

Nothing has ever been seen so clearly by my mind's eye, I think. I still know the simplicity and the yellowish shadows in the whorls of its surface, and my hand behind it with the skin infinitely crude and coarse and lined, the fresh palm of a child.

I held the thing carefully for what were probably only a few seconds. I recognized it fully, without any doubt or timidity, as my own soul. Then I put it gently into my mouth, bit into it, and chewed and swallowed it.

It had nothing to do with food or even nourishment, being without taste, and moist, but at the same time almost floury.

I made sure that none had stayed in my mouth and that all of it was well down my throat, for it was important that it reassemble itself and stay there inside me, to grow. I knew that I would see it again, just as I knew that something very important had happened to me, perhaps the first since being born. It was in a way like becoming a person instead of a creature, woman instead of baby, big instead of little. I was myself, *me,* and I had seen and touched the proof of it. I had been shown.

The good day unfolded like all other days before me, the happy child, but of course I was different, for I had a core now.

For many years, I occasionally remembered this, but without any questioning at all. I never wondered about its next visit, but I knew there would be one, just as I knew that people would tell me it was a little accident of bodily secretion or digestion, or a dream, if I talked of it.

But the night that it did come again was a mistake, except for the reassurance that it was still there.

It was as if I thought this occasion unworthy of it. I was befouled by fever; the different parts of me seemed to be sending off almost visible fumes and stinking gases, when I would choose to be silk and sweet oils for it. The rats were behind it, trailing their shreds of my tissue, my lining, my guts, and still ripping and gnawing at me with their filthy teeth as I coughed passionately in the middle of the black room by my bed. It was ugly, my state.

"Go back," I screamed, as my soul rose like a smooth nut in my throat.

It had grown since our first meeting. Some of the convolutions of its polished carving had worn even fainter since I'd seen it like a little quiet keepsake in my hand, pearly but not gleaming, wet but not slippery, ivory colored but not dull.

It sickened me that I must ask it to return to the bloody mob below, yet I knew with all my tattered force that it was not yet time to hold it in my hand again, and that I could not do so with dignity.

There was no clash of wills between us, certainly, but I learned something of eternity before it did withdraw.

I hate to think of it then in the red caves and the long flaming tunnels, for that was a bad night for it and me.

The next day I asked for help, being in a state of exhaustion that I could never try to explain to anyone. A professionally kind stranger came and left some advice and some fresh courage, and the Achromycin pills in a little bottle, to drive out the mouse in my left lung.

I felt sorry about that. But it was the mouse or me, the doctor said, and I am important because the next time my soul shows up, I must be in good shape to welcome it. I may be very old, with no teeth to chew it, no juice left to swallow it, but I shall catch it in the palm of my hand as I did when I was a child, and this time let it lead me.

—*St. Helena, California, 1965*

7

A Few of the Men

Any confession of love, especially a shameless one, is an open bid for speculation from the curious, the jealous, and even the malicious. There is some trace of all this in my own self, as I set forth in public, after long private consideration, what I think about a few of the men in my life.

How best to name them in cold print, and deliberately, is really a question of loyalty. It is a mean choosy business, to narrow to a handful the list of one's true loves. Half of the ones in my life, perhaps fortunately, have existed wholly or in part on paper and in ink. A few still do: in and on my reading conscience.

Jean-Anthelme Brillat-Savarin, for instance, lived in the flesh as surely as did Sam Ward. Sherlock Holmes and Inspector Maigret, on the contrary, are chemically compounded of wood pulp and printers' blood. My feelings for them are equally real. I know what they look and sound like, and how they think, and even what they like to eat and wear, as clearly as if I had lived alongside all of them.

Of course there is a small something of both awe and sisterliness in all such relationships as the ones I must have with my real loves. It has since the first been necessary for me to feel shy and basically inexperienced, pupil and not teacher, with the men in my life, whether of the mind or the body. How could I not feel awe, in my long close knowledge of Brillat-Savarin, nor a certain amount of warm tolerant sibling love for Inspector Maigret, whose drinking has sometimes worried me and whose wife often bores me a little, in a familial way?

Brillat-Savarin lived from April 1, 1755, to February 2, 1826 —long for those days—and his classic *Physiology of Taste* was published anonymously a few months before he died. It was his only literary offspring, and his only self-portrait in a mysteriously reticent lifetime as an obscure Parisian lawyer.

Samuel Ward was born in New York City on January 27, 1814, when Brillat-Savarin was getting along in years, at three in the afternoon. This was "the fashionable hour for dinner," it is noted by Lately Thomas, whose biography of Ward is new and definitive. "Promptness at mealtimes was to be a characteristic of the new arrival through a long and eventful life." My dear Sam died on May 19, 1884, leaving hundreds of letters and poems to reveal his warmth and brilliance, through a wild and often shady career as Washington lobbyist and charming rascal.

Sherlock Holmes was born, full-fledged of course, from the head of the Scottish Jupiter Dr. Arthur Conan Doyle, in 1887, in *A Study in Scarlet.* Then from 1891 until his *Return,* his astounding imperturbability developed into an international and probably indestructible legend, as he solved hideous as well as voluptuous crimes from his "bachelor flat" in Baker Street, London. He is undoubtedly one of the most *tangible* imaginary human beings of this present world.

As for Inspector Maigret, he was born as far as I am concerned in about 1930, although he was probably then in his early thirties himself. I began a long liaison with him that year, through Georges Simenon's almost uncountable series of books about his adventures with the French police. Maigret was somewhat younger then he is now, although not the decades that calendars would indicate, and he has been getting a little slower and heavier physically, being as human as anyone else. When last I met him in print, he was seriously considering retirement, an intolerable prospect from any point of view. Both his wife and I fret about this.

And here is an emotional hazard one runs with modern creators of men like Maigret. Simenon, for instance, is almost uncomfortably realistic, so that one must accept with resignation the thickening waistlines and the thinning hairs on the printed page, which one also faces in actuality. Dr. Doyle's Sherlock Holmes, in comparison, is unreal. His worshippers have done all they can to make him human, and the Baker Street Irregulars, both actual and wishful, have evolved desperate little familiarities with his personal habits. Nothing really makes him, however, anything but an archhuman, untouchable, just as he is/was an archmisogynist. It would be an impertinence, for instance, to think of him as bilious, or thirsty or sweaty, as I know Sam Ward and Maigret and even Brillat-Savarin must often have been.

There are many fine aspects about the long affairs I have carried on with all these men. One is that they can be managed synonymously, without travail or guilt, and can warm me in their own ways without any quarrel of the mind or heart. Another is that I can accept with equanimity the cold fact that probably not one of the lot would have given me a second look. Thus I can snoop into their affairs with detachment, immunity, appreciation . . . and no feeling of personal involvement.

Of course Mr. Holmes had Dr. Watson to watch over him: friend, buffer, stooge. And Maigret has Madame Maigret, a fine woman of whom I am fond. She is perfect for him: devoted, practical, patient, a good cook, and above all kind, although like Dr. Watson she is inclined to fuss about things like wearing an overcoat in bad weather.

It is different with Sam Ward, and I must confess to a more active personal curiosity about his two beautiful wives and what I know in my heart was a life filled with the skilled appreciation of witty sexy fascinating women everywhere. Perhaps (and a tentacle of my nature curls around this prospect), he might have found me worth at least one fleeting but pleased glance?

As for Brillat-Savarin, in many ways he affects me as Sam does: I accept the plain fact that his interest in me would be casual and possibly cool, except across the dining table, but still I feel a lively, personal, but unpossessive curiosity about the women he did know.

He was always attractive physically, even when old. "A man of great wit," his friend Dr. Richerand wrote, "a most agreeable dinner companion, and one endowed with measureless gaiety, he was the center of attraction in any gathering fortunate enough to have his company, for he gave himself up willingly to the seductions of worldly society, and only spurned them when he could delight in the more intimate pleasures of true friendship."

There's the man for me. I first met him when I was perhaps twenty. I was living with a family in Dijon, where my husband and I were going to the university. Madame Ollagnier was an almost pathologically stingy woman who still managed to set a good table, with the help of a series of terrified slaveys and the firm gastronomical demands of her architect husband. We ate well, twice a day, and occasionally with what Dr. George Saintsbury would call supernacular finesse.

Once, and I believe it was to celebrate the end of Lent in 1931, the dull wine carafe was not on the table at noon, nor was there any sign of the water that we were urged to use "for reasons of health" to dilute our subordinary Burgundy. Instead there were two dusty bottles: exciting, encouraging! And with ceremony a cobwebbed and indeed moldy casserole was produced reverently from the tiny kitchen, and Monsieur Ollagnier informed us with a flourish of trumpets in his voice that it was from Belley.

He was a tactful man. Undoubtedly he sensed our timid ignorance of why the origin of this odd blue-green-gray dish should ring bells, and he told us deftly that Belley was the birthplace of Jean-Anthelme Brillat-Savarin, one of the glories of France. Then with a dramatic shrug, implying that our own minds must take over from there, he plunged his two knives along the edge of the mildewed crust.

"This pâté has spent at least a year on the shelf in the cellar of a distant cousin of mine, who carries on the classical traditions of the region," he said. "It will have shaped itself into a miracle of flavor. Once correctly served, as is its due," and here he lifted off the whole crust with a surgical flourish and tossed it disdainfully onto a platter Madame held for him, in a shower of pure penicillin culture, "and after we have had a few sips of these slightly weary but still robust Arbois, served in honor of the sainted lawyer, gastronomer, raconteur par excellence, and amateur physiologist, we will sit here until we have eaten this whole damned pâté, for to expose it more than a few hours to the open air would be a sacrilege, an infamous desecration."

And this we did, for a luncheon lasting perhaps four hours, when even Madame stopped counting the wattage of the light that burned above us in the hideous little dank dark room. We protected the Belley masterpiece from ignominy, and did away with at least three long loaves of bread and two batches of salad, and of course the first two bottles of wine from Brillat-Savarin's general district and a couple more, and when I finally confessed that I had never heard any of the names before, Monsieur Ollagnier said scornfully that many Frenchmen never had either, which I find to be true to this day.

As we went on rescuing the pâté, and toasting almost everything that came to mind, he told me many things that I later found to be incorrect, but that gave a good picture of the somewhat shadowy old lawyer who startled all his friends by publishing, a few months before his death, *La Physiologie du goût*. Apparently I fell in love then, that day of the massive mildewed dish, but the affair really did not take shape until I was almost accidentally talked into making a new translation of his odd book.

I was composing an anthology of great feasts, and I found myself affronted by the awkward English versions of the *Physiology*. "I can do better," I protested, and I added that this and that should not have happened to such clear delightful prose. "Then why don't you?" I was asked coldly. So for about two years I lived, as closely as human beings can live with the printed word, in the mind, the life, the world of this wonderful old man.

As a matter of fact, there are conflicting reports on whether he *was* wonderful. Certainly his Paris set was amazed when he quietly produced a small classic. His admiring young friend Richerand wrote well of him, but other people did not; he was described disdainfully as an oaf, a hulking tall figure in the courts of law who often carried dead birds in his coattails to hasten their gaminess for a dinner dish.

It is a dubious thing about his being married, but I do not care. Certainly it is too bad that if he had a wife, he did not want to show her to his friends. He wrote of himself as a bachelor, perhaps wishfully, and it was not until more than fifty years after he died that Charles Monselet stated, upon talking with many people who still remembered him (How many are there now, who can remember a modest man dead that long?), "His widow lived long after him." I think she was a relative of one of his brothers, but a pleasant facet of the love life of the intellect is that this does not matter, least of all to me, the faithful one.

Brillat-Savarin enjoyed the company of his cousin Juliette Recamier, as did many other men of her time. I admire his taste here, without any cavil except about the rumor of her reluctant virginity: he, and she too, might have been happier otherwise.

It is also rumored that in America about 1795, when he was a dashing young refugee playing his violin and appreciating the virtues and accents of his female language students, he may possibly have fathered a child who became one of the ancestors of S. L. M. Barlow, trusted intimate of my friend Sam Ward! Descendants of Barlow regretfully deny that there is any branch of the family tree on which to perch a by-blow of the professor, but at least he and Barlow and Ward himself all shared knowledge of the good things in life.

My first meeting with Sam was when I read *Oscar Wilde Discovers America,* shortly after it was published in 1936. (There, I thought, is a man for me!) In 1882, when Ward introduced young Wilde with glitter and fanfare but withal respect to the voracity of American society, Sam was a ripe but seething sixty-eight, much beloved and despised and already something of a legend on both sides of the Atlantic . . . "delicious uncle," he was called, "the Universal Uncle" . . .

(I am interested to note that while I savor his avuncular reputation, and agree with its many merits, I cannot but feel that it overlaid, as it were, his true nature as a Complete Man, aware sexually in the right way always, whether he beamed upon a homesick grandchild in London or wrote a wittily effusive love lyric to Lillie Langtry in New York.)

My second meeting with this wonderful rogue, crook, con-noisseur, wit, linguist, bandit, counterspy, gastronomer, political reprobate, and all the other things he has deservedly been called by his exasperated and adoring relatives, friends, and enemies, was when I had the chance to correspond about him with Lately Thomas. Again there was instant recognition; plainly I am at-tracted, like many women, to the rascal saints . . .

Of course Sherlock Holmes will always remain beyond this dar-ing familiarity. He was born about thirty years before my own birth in 1908, and when I first met him, during a bout of measles at the age of eight, he shifted easily into a father image. Holmes was thin and tall like my sire Rex Kennedy, and as far as I can tell he wore the same tall thin nose. (Here the image confuses itself with Basil Rathbone, the consummate portrait of the other two men: Basil-Rex-Sherlock-Rathbone-Kennedy-Holmes.)

My father, of course, never sawed away at the violin in mo-ments of fleeting perplexity, as did Holmes, nor call out occasion-ally for a deft application of "the needle." There remains in me to this day, however, a feeling of daughterly devotion to them both, and one I could not shake off if I wanted to. This means, naturally, that there is a touch of awe in it, and that is right too: I can still flinch as any good child should before the slightly scornful impatience, the veiled sneer, in Basil-Sherlock-Rex's remote voice as he/they touched on some imbecility of mine.

Once past my first view, absorbed and naive, of the various shoddy volumes that now make up *The Complete Sherlock Holmes,* I felt at home. Reading steadily, in bed and with a fever, is an act that can make any tale burn into one's heart. I learned this for all my life when I was eight, and have often seized the chance since then, and when next I picked up the thread with serious intent, some thirty years later, I was at home again.

This was when I suddenly knew that my mind needed a purge. I had been working and living and even thinking too fast. As instinctively as a constipated cat seeks out tender grass stalks, I put *Sherlock Holmes* by my bed, and looked at nothing else ever printed until I had chewed my way amiably, contentedly, through *A Study in Scarlet, The Sign of Four, The Adventures of Sherlock Holmes, The Memoirs of Sherlock Holmes, The Return of Sherlock Holmes, The Hound of the Baskervilles, The Valley of Fear, His Last Bow,* and *The Case Book of Sherlock Holmes.* I arose resigned, as after a restorative and leisurely feast with rare friends.

I doubt that I picked up any mannerisms from this prolonged intimacy, as writers and lovers are in danger of doing, but I felt, and still feel, that I learned many ways *not* to do and be, much as a child who hears correct grammar does not split infinitives nor say "he don't." There is something exciting and cleansing about even a page or two of Arthur Conan Doyle's fast simple unadorned prose. Logic is there, far stronger than any ridiculous cliff-hanging, but the real medicine, especially for a person like me, inclined to involved and occasionally shaky syntax, is the complete plainness of the prose. There is no nonsense about it, and yet it is magically romantic, in the best sense.

As for my first meeting with Inspector Maigret, I owe it to my younger sister Norah, unwitting entrepreneur, who in 1931 was fourteen years old and living with me in France.

I had got her into a bit of trouble at the convent by encouraging her to read a copy of Colette's *L'Envers de music-hall* as an example of good tight French. The mother superior was horrified. I cast about for some substitute, and with almost the same felicity started my sister on Georges Simenon, this time more discreetly. His books were easy to buy in railroad stations, and were cheap, like Colette's. I worried a little because he encouraged Norah to use dots instead of more classical punctuation, but at least she knew what they stood for, and his past subjunctive was impeccable. Of course I read the dots, and verbs and what went along with all of them, and realized quite soon that I would be happy if I could spend the rest of my life with Monsieur Maigret, Simenon's fabulous creature. And I have done so.

Ours is a comfortable relationship. There is naturally a certain amount of sex in it, but this is no menace to any of us, including Madame. I feel at ease with them both, not daughterly surely but without any need to try to interrupt their fine marital pattern. Maigret has taught me a great deal, like all the others. In his case it is not so much a question of syntax and logic, as it is of being with other humans. His understanding of them, and his quiet wise tolerance, have been good for me. And through him I have of course been able to meet many people I most probably could never have known otherwise—just as Mr. Holmes introduced me long ago to "a gigantic hound," "a lady dressed in black and heavily veiled," and to the archdevil Professor Moriarty himself.

Oftener than not, the most interesting people in Maigret's adventures are corpses, but very soon I am led expertly to see why, which in turn makes many other things plainer to me in the outside world.

The people Sam Ward has introduced me to, on the other hand, (even Oscar Wilde!) tend to look pale beside Sam's own dapper and usually well-fed image. I am a little shy before them, bedazzled by their cleverness and their worldly glow. Sam is enough for me.

This fading of the background is not true of Brillat-Savarin. I warm to every person in his life, with and through him. With Sam I actually see only Sam, but with the old French lawyer I am in a world that is as much mine as his, because of the way he reveals it to me. I know Juliette Recamier, the teaser, and young Dr. Riche-

rand who ate too fast, and the two old brothers Dubois who could
never eat too much.

The brothers were seventy-eight and seventy-six, ancients in
those days of early mortality: "freshly shaved, their hair carefully
arranged and well-powdered, two little old men who were still spry
and healthy." They invited themselves to breakfast one morning,
sharply at ten, and began with two dozen oysters each, "and a
gleaming golden lemon," washed down with plenty of sauternes.
Then grilled skewered kidneys were served, a pâté of truffled foie
gras *en croûte,* and finally the cheese fondue that the brothers had
expressly asked for, a recipe their host had learned while he was a
refugee in Switzerland. After the fondue came fresh fruits and
sweetmeats, coffee, and "finally two kinds of liqueur, one sharp
for refreshing the palate and the other oily for soothing it."

The three gentlemen then took a gentle constitutional around
the apartment. It was discovered to be two o'clock, the correct
dinner hour in those days, and without any real protest the brothers Dubois "seated themselves, pulled nearer to the table, spread
out their napkins, and prepared for action."

After the unexpected but delectable meal that Brillat-Savarin
and his cook managed to turn out (thanks to their own resources
and some help from restaurants in the neighborhood), my friend
introduced the newfangled idea of a cup of tea to the old fellows,
and they enjoyed several rounds of it by the hearth. And then,
without more than lip protest, they shared a bowl of hot rum
punch and one plateful and then another of "beautifully thin,
delicately buttered, and perfectly salted slices of toast" . . . and it
was past eight o'clock and never one dull moment, thanks to the
subtle and untiring attentions my dear professor paid to his two
ancient and delighted guests. The next day they reported by note
to him that "after the sweetest of sleeps [they] had arisen re-
freshed, feeling both able and eager to begin anew."

This warms my heart: tact, interest, complete generosity. So, in much the same way, does Thomas's account of the time when Sam Ward was an old man in London and cheered a lonely suffering little granddaughter in Brown's Hotel by sending her a surprise bundle every few minutes (a beautiful ring, an elegant traveling case, baskets of ripe fruit) before she sailed to America to die— which perhaps because of his magic she did not do for many decades.

Sherlock Holmes did many small kind things too, generous and warm behind their sardonic restraint, and of course Inspector Maigret is the epitome of gruff kindliness, capable of true compassion. He, like all the other men, has the gift of making people *trust* him, even in his detested role of cop, judge and jury, and occasional executioner.

After the years and the lives I have shared with these four people, they are clearer to my mind's eye than many I saw this morning, and clearer than any picture could ever paint them. The nearest thing to a good portrait of Maigret is the blocklike silhouette of a slouched hat brim, a pipe between thick firm lips, a jutting nose that advertises most of the paperbacks about him. This does not bother me at all. I know better, just as I know old Sam Ward because and then in spite of every cartoon and photograph of him, bloated, corrupt, always dapper.

Sherlock Holmes is of course inextricably composed for me of my father's graceful lankiness and long nose, with Rathbone in there for the right curl to the lips.

As for Jean-Anthelme Brillat-Savarin, little need be thought about his personal appearance. He was variously described by some of his contemporaries, but I myself know that he was a tall healthy man, fastidious in spite of what might be warming in his coattails, with a tendency to corpulence, which he diagnosed and coped with, wearing his own scientifically designed corset when other efforts failed.

Perhaps the most rewarding thing about all these love affairs that I have kept up so enjoyably for so long is that, except for Maigret, I know and accept how the gentlemen died. Few women can say this with equanimity.

There are a few accounts of the last moments of good and even bad men that never fail to move me to actual tears, whether or not I loved either the writer or the person whose death made the words ring with the adequate poignancy. This is true, somewhat to my surprise, when I read of Sam Ward's dying: I am physically moved. I am there in the villa in Italy, in May of 1884. The old man is very ill, perhaps from a Carnaval feast of "succulent steamed mussels" in Naples with an old friend. Sam is awake, breathing heavily. He dictates a wryly jaunty letter. Then, fixing his always brilliant eyes upon us, he says clearly, "I think I am going to give up the ghost." (And here I must steel myself, as I have in my life before . . .) And with a long sigh he is gone. In the next room his niece Daisy weeps. Beneath his pillow is the dog-eared Horace, and on the bedspread beside him, Khayyám, open at Omar's envoi:

> *And when like her, O Saki, you shall pass*
> *Among the Guests Star-scattered on the Grass,*
>   *And in your joyous errand reach the spot*
> *Where I made One—turn down an empty Glass!*

I weep here. Every time I must weep a little, and Sam would like that. But one cannot feed too often on such helpless tears, and I am glad Maigret has not yet brought me to them. He is getting on, but I do not fear for him in my own lifetime.

As for Sherlock Holmes, I suffered along with myriad others when he and Professor Moriarty died together in the Reichenbach Fall, and then I returned to a confident acceptance of his immortality long before he himself did a quick jump back into print. He *Return*ed. Naturally. I knew he would when I was eight years old, and I still do.

Perhaps it is odd that the proof of Brillat-Savarin's command of my love is that I can read of his death, and think upon it, with complete serenity. He taught me how.

He died fairly quickly of simple pneumonia, contracted after an obligatory attendance at a chilly mass for the repose of the soul of Louis XVI, for which and for whom he felt small reverence. His relative and godson Dr. Recamier attended him, and noted that he seemed to understand that his end was upon him. He waited for it without regret, for his writings proved that he had long looked upon death with the same philosophical detachment he felt toward life. One of his admirers wrote, "He left the world like a satisfied diner leaving the banquet-room . . ."

It interests me, and may even lead some to the speculation that this type of confession can, that at least two of the main men in my life are detectives. Jacques Barzun, in his introduction to *The Delights of Detection,* says that "the emotion called forth [by detective feats] is that of seeing order grow out of confusion." This is something, of course, that gives courage and reassurance to no matter what type of woman, and I feel especially sensitive to it because of my wishful dependence upon a better order than my own.

Dr. Barzun goes on to describe a detective as "a man of independent mind, an eccentric possibly, something of an artist even in his scientific work, and in any case a creature of will and scope superior to the crowd. He is, in short, the last of the heroes."

Yes, of course: that is it! Here is Everyman; here are all of them, sleuths or not, and it is plain that I have openly searched all my life, or at least since I was a measly eight, for a hero. How amazing, how undeservedly rewarding, to have found at least four to lean on forever!

From Mr. Holmes I have learned the virtues, if not the practice, of being succinct. From Inspector Maigret have come a deepened patience and compassion, and from Sam Ward, "delicious uncle," has flowed over me the meaning of human gaiety, for he was, in both the catholic and the Catholic sense, debonair. Longest and best of all my learning has come from Brillat-Savarin: delicate discretion, warmly conceived and practiced, always beyond my common grasp, never to be feared or disdained. I am rich to have known these gentlemen, and to remain faithful to them after my fashion.

—*St. Helena, California, 1965*

8

The Blue Gun

This may not be an extraordinary experience, but I think it is at least unusual, that a person can actually experience death in a dream. I did, nearly twice. This time I seemed reticent, or perhaps cautious, about the final bliss I had felt the first time.

I was almost asleep tonight, lying on my left side, waiting without impatience for my night life to begin. Suddenly I was recollecting, but without meaning to, a dream I had completely forgotten in my waking life, one I had had perhaps a week or a few nights ago. I knew that I was merely remembering and that I was not redreaming. I did not question, but I was conscious that this was a strange occurrence.

The second time, it was the actual dying that was important, much like the last chapter of a well-remembered novel. I felt the hole form around the bullet as it entered the base of my skull and proceeded firmly up toward the right eye socket. Then, deliberately but with no fear, I stopped the thing, wakened myself, and for a time was in full possession of the first dream, of which this was the rear end. Already it fades, but a wonder remains.

In the beginning I was a fictional woman, having an affair with a strong, vicious or at least ruthless man. We decided to kill his wife, and got a beautiful little gun. It was blue, I think, a little toy.

Then she was sitting at a table, her back to a low stone wall, and she became me, as behind her/me the man spoke over the wall, framed in dappled sunlight and leaves and flowers and as from a gladsome pergola. He said that he had decided to kill me instead.

I turned slowly and saw the gun. I knew it was my turn to die, and at once. I felt a flash of fear, but only a flash, and a question about how long it would hurt, but there was no time for protest.

I leaned a little forward on the table, which was the stone one I once sat at in a garden in Provence. "Look," I had said jokingly that day. "There is my typewriter and I am writing a book, a really beautiful one, a masterpiece!"

Behind me now I knew the little blue gun in the dappled light was aiming. I did not hear it fire, but as I dropped lazily onto the table, the hole at the base of my skull formed itself to welcome the bullet, which traveled in an almost leisurely way toward my right eye socket. I was somewhat surprised at the obvious path it took, and at the general lack of confusion. I had guessed there might be lightning or ugly noises, but the only positive thing was its irrevocability: it was an accomplished fact.

When the bullet was about halfway through my head, I began to fade, or rather there was a strong cloudiness that seemed to spread out from the bullet. I was almost dead. There was no fear or pain. In another inch, I was almost formless, a log, a great mist. It was a merging of my identity with nonidentity, and never had I been so real, so vast, so meaningless. I disappeared, and the bullet no doubt emerged through the right eye socket, but it did not matter to anything.

—St. Helena, California, 1966

9

Paris

The old man was reading a current magazine devoted, that month, to Paris. "This is supposed to be about Paris," he said. I asked him three times, "Does it make you want to go back, does it make you want to go *back,* DOES IT MAKE YOU—" "No," he said with dignity. Then he added cynically, "Love in Paris, this and that in Paris! Hah. One thing, dining and dancing—that does interest one a little—"

I thought of his obviously dogged efforts to down something, anything, at table. I thought of his belchings and hackings.

And then I thought of the last time I was in Paris with him. We were staying at a small old hotel beside the Continental, and could walk a few steps and dodge a few cabs and be in the Tuileries. We could go down some graceful steps, the kind architects would put in an opera house or a luxury liner for ladies to float down in fabulous gowns, and we would be on the hard-packed earth of the gardens, with flashing tiny sails visible to our left from the round pond and the haunting wails of the Punch-and-Judy shows to our right, and before us, topless towers, Paris, blue air, bliss.

One day we walked down the little dingy street. It was about three o'clock, I think. We had lunched in the back room of the Café de la Paix—lots of caviar and lots of iced vodka, and then, as I remember, artichokes and then Turkish coffee, a strange good meal. Edith (my mother and his wife) felt weary. She lay down on the elaborate brass bed. I pulled the cherry-colored satin puff over her, and she smiled in a gay knowing way at me and closed her eyes. We went down in the gilt-wire elevator, a shaky little cage, to the drab street that let so abruptly onto the almost intolerable gaiety of the Tuileries—yes, gay and tender with that ineffable and perhaps aphrodisiacal blue to it.

I don't remember anything except feeling free, with the caviar and vodka and pungent coffee in me and the warmth of my mother's smile, until we got to those steps, the ones that go down from the street. My father strode along in his monumental way. I think we talked about breakfasts, and about one he had vanquished that morning in the Anglican catacombs of the Continental, across the street from our hotel. I have a feeling of midafternoon noise, the honkings and clackings.

Then we were halfway down those wonderful steps. Light flashed on the sails on the pond far to our left. Taxis bleated behind us. The trees trembled like a sea, and up from their shade came the treble of a thousand children's voices. Space, space . . .

My father, a tall man dressed outlandishly and beautifully in white linen, with a wide Panama on his fine beaky head, waved his cane, which he used only outside the boundaries of the United States, and cried out, far over the Tuileries, the flowing river Seine, the Left Bank, perhaps even backward to the room where his wife lay dozing, a big triumphant shout, with the cane lifted and the beaky head back; *"God,* but I feel good."

It was possibly the best I have ever heard his voice. It was everything I wanted anyone I love to feel in Paris.

It would be impossible for me ever to recount the ways I have existed in that place. I have told a few. But one thing I can repeat, that when my youngest sister and my brother, she twenty and he eighteen I believe, came there and I met them, while I was living in Switzerland, I said to my husband, "Oh, I could weep for them —it is not the beautiful place it was when I first came to it in 1929. The quays have changed, trees are down, the taxis all have tops— oh, no!" He looked at me in a remote smiling way and said, "I once could have wept for you. Nineteen twenty-nine! What a crude year! You did not know Paris when it was Paris, in 1915, when I came back after seventeen days at the front and the janitor of the little Hôtel Foyot above the restaurant cut off my boots and bathed me and after I had slept for twenty hours brought me a bowl of wild strawberries. No, poor you. You never knew—and your brother and sister will pity their youngsters just as you and I . . ."

That is true. It has happened. By now I am pitying my children, and at the same time my heart is thick with envy, to be them, to be in Paris for the first time. I would once more be my father, so tall and complete, raising his cane against the pale sky and shouting out in the freest gesture of his life, "God, but I feel good." I would be my mother, under the satin coverlet, smiling so wisely. I would be that husband, arriving there wet and weary and finally fed by a gentle furnace man. I would be me, yes, in Paris, I would be me.

—St. Helena, California, 1969

10

The Green Talk

Two nights ago I worked for a long time, mostly in my subconscious, I suppose, on finding out about the Green Talk.

In my dream, the Green Talk was in the same class with ESP, and the ability to use it varied with people, so that June Eddy, for instance, could speak the Green Talk more easily and naturally than could I or Joe Abegg, or other people I was apparently concerned with that night.

If a person has any capacity for it at all—and most of us live and die unaware of it—it can be consciously developed, through exercise directed by someone who has the gift strongly. Apparently it is best to live very closely with such a person in order to attain any skill. For instance, married people often have the Green Talk.

In itself, the Green Talk is the ability to speak without sound —a kind of transference of speech from one spirit to another. When people use it well, questions can be asked and answered without any physical contact: expressions in the eyes or mouth, touch, or of course sound. What is best, and rarest, is that long and witty conversations can go on, between two or more people who have the gift for Green Talk and who have exercised it deliberately—*practiced,* that is.

I cannot remember from the dream whether it is used in prisons, but I rather think so, if the right people are confined together long enough (as in marriage?!)

In the dream (it has already lost its sharp edges, but the fact that I still think about parts of it makes it worth holding on to), I had enough of a gift for the Green Talk to work on it, and several friends helped me. As I became more at ease with it, through their gently patient help in communicating, I felt an increasing sense of pleasure. It was delightful to be in communication with other minds that attracted mine. Of course, this idea that there are two or three levels of speech that can go on in one person has often been written about—I think of a long play by Eugene O'Neill— but I don't remember ever hearing about the Green Talk. In that old play, which interested me very much when I saw and then read it, the third language existed solely within the person who spoke it. The Green Talk, in contrast, is strictly for communication between two or more people. It is not at all secret, and can be picked up by anyone who knows it—or rather, who is aware that it is being spoken and who can go along . . .

I am sure that at its best, it can be used by two skilled people at long distance, much as letters can be exchanged, or voice by telephone or wireless or satellite. In my dream, my own experiments were limited by my fumbling ignorance of the potential within me, and I had to be in the same room or garden or elevator in order to speak it, even with a person much more in control than I. There was no need for any physical contact, although apparently there had to be sympathy, even love—and of course familiarity.

Once this invisible contact was established, no matter how

clumsily, I had an almost exalted feeling of enjoyment, of success, of having grown a little farther past the terrible blind limitations of *matter*.

There is no doubt that this feeling of having opened one more tiny door is attained in true meditation, which of course takes great self-discipline and training. It is an inner triumph, and one that I know only indirectly, except for a few instants of realization that flashed upon me and then past me as if to show what *could* be done. But the Green Talk is not meant for anything but communication. In my dream, there was no fear that it would or could be abused, as the telephone can be. The Green Talk is not an instrument but a way . . . and it interested me, even as my subconscious explored it a little, that I could recognize my own limits of attainment. There was no false modesty about this, any more than there is when I know that my skills as a writer, by now developed about as far as they can be, are infinitely smaller than many people's. In the dream, June, for instance, was so much more at ease with the Green Talk than I could ever be that I felt a warm deep gratitude for her for even bothering to help me stumble along. It was rather like a dialogue between Gandhi and a first-year Methodist minister . . . between Einstein and a high school math teacher. But there was nothing but gentle patience toward me as a learner, and June and several other people helped me slowly to speak the Green Talk. My sister Anne was there for a while; several other people I have known, and many I have never consciously met before, began to communicate easily but in what I knew was a simplified way with me.

Always there was the feeling of joyfulness.

I don't know why this form of inaudible invisible conversation is called the Green Talk, but all the time I was dreaming, I kept reminding myself to hang on to the name, to remember it deliberately in the flash before consciousness, and to repeat it sternly because of its terrible importance. This I did, even while I tried to continue the dream explanation. (This process, often used by deliberate dreamers, is much like trying to prolong and hold on to a sexual orgasm, I think.)

Why "green"? Why "talk," even?

To answer that last question, the communication was clearly in words, phrases, sentences. It was not simply a wordless understanding, the kind often experienced even by dull people—the rush of love or compassion, the fleeting exchange of recognition that often flows between people in buses, on streets, in beds. The Green Talk was *talk,* but it was silent.

It went on, perhaps, in the same way that a skilled pianist will play on a silent keyboard while he travels in a plane or bus, or even will move his fingers in his sleep to the sounds his mind conjures. The Green Talk could be carried on at a large dinner party, in a quiet room where only two or three worked or sat or lay, or in a crowded public place. But it took two people. That is perhaps the crux of it—two or, sometimes in my dream, several. And it need not be an urgent communication. Indeed, it was simply a higher form of inter-talk than most of us are aware of.

And I was the novice, plainly touched by the gift but in a very simple and crude way. I stumbled along, and felt happy and excited. It was one more way to be sensate, *awake,* even if in a dream.

—St. Helena, California, 1971

11

Strip Search

The question on a talk show was about how and why and if women should be stripped and searched by the police. Men were mentioned too, of course, and a few called the station. One said he thought men enjoyed it, and another said that men are used to being naked on command, in locker rooms for athletics and in enlistment centers and things like that. One man said he found his one strip search traumatic and afterward felt as if he had been raped.

But all the breathless trembling women who called, no matter how skilled at being breathless etc., sounded violently outraged.

Most of them, and this was the problem of the show's hostess, too, had been submitted to the search unjustly, for ridiculous things like letting a dog out without a leash or for signing a small check knowing that it could not be paid at once.

Of course I think such invasion of privacy is outrageous, unless public safety is involved.

Some of the police and some of the male callers argued that lice and other social varmints were taken care of in such searches. This was done by means of an injected spray of chemicals, without the victim's permission, in "the public good."

Well, I listened and sympathized here and there, as is usually the case with such shows and especially with certain hosts I have come to recognize since I read less. (Progressive cataracts on both eyes, and I manage to listen at night while I prepare vegetables and so on for the next day's meals . . . it is an agreeable schedule.)

Yes, I said, when the voice asked in a hard way, "Has this ever happened to you?" Yes, it did once. But I know that I was a very fortunate person, because it did not hurt my amour-propre at all, and I felt there was no real outrage to my private self; my main feeling was one of great compassion for the policewoman who had to do it to me.

This reaction may sound very sanctimonious and holier than thou and a lot of other revolting things, but it is true. I still feel sorry for the officer who had to do it to me. I know that she was required to do it, and at the same time I know how it would be if it happened to me in another time and place, for instance, with male cops watching on closed-circuit TV in case the female examiners "needed help."

Well, I had nobody, either. But I did not need anything but my own self-control, as it turned out, and my firm wish not to yawn.

It was at Heathrow, an airport that has never been even amiable to me. It had started several days earlier, when I told a travel agent very firmly, down in Marseille, that I did not want to travel on a DC-10, either from Marseille to Paris or from Paris to London or, most especially, from London to Los Angeles. For one reason or another, though, I was on this abominable wide-bodied piece of airborne cardboard and chewing gum, and I sat back like a fatalistic Fury past anger, as we jiggled in and out of airports. It seemed always to be the same plane, but of course we had a new set of stewardesses now and then, so I knew to look for rest rooms in different places.

Finally, on the last leg, somewhere over the North Sea, the lights blinked out several times and a pale-lipped stewardess made a little joke about candlelight dinners as she tried to fit a plastic tray over my middle, and then dropped her flashlight as we went into real dark. Across from me a tiny dark man, who was buckled into his double-width seat with his legs crossed, was praying to Allah. He was the prime minister of some eastern kingdom, and behind him sat his empress, a tall Paris model, and back from her in the other "class" were about thirty of their servants and a couple of little princesses. Most of them praying too, I felt sure.

So we got back to Heathrow, after dumping almost all the fuel into the North Sea and being refused permission to land in Ireland. We went in sideways, to the middle of a field of brussels sprouts, with lights playing on us and ambulances winking. It was nice to see lights again. The trip had been bumpy, dark, and cold, since everything was off or out except the quiet voice of the prime minister, saying in an almost conversational chant, Allah . . . Allah . . . Allalalalah . . .

When the lights went on, once we were quiet in the little cabbages, I looked at him, almost dozing in his double seat, a tiny tired old man. Behind him the beautiful empress looked straight at me. We did not smile or nod, but there was an instant of complete communication.

In the airport we stood in a lengthy line, and I saw long rods being held out toward us as we shuffled past officers and guards. We were tired. We were taken to a shoddily bright and elegant hotel at the airport, and I remember taking a long shower in a shoddy elegant room. Then I lay on sheets starched to make them seem thicker, but clean ones, until in about two hours I was summoned to return to the airport for takeoff. I think we had breakfast first in a big restaurant that must look the same way all day and all night. There were big buses outside, and when I told a driver or somebody who was getting us into one that I had two bags and did not see them, he patted my shoulder and said, "Daountcha worry, luv," in such a soft nice way that I almost fell onto his shapely small shoulder with happy reassurance. I still feel warmed by his voice.

Once in the business part of Heathrow, though, things were cold and crisp, and there we all were again, like herded sheep, shuffling slowly toward a row of officers and desks and guards. I paid little heed. I felt fatalistic, victimized, invaded. There was no way to escape the lines, the eyes looking, the ghastly politeness. We shuffled toward the place where the desks were, and facing them to our left were the men with the cattle prods or whatever they were, darting and weaving them indirectly at our pockets and our minds and our even more private parts.

Two men ahead of me was a well-dressed youngish man whom I'd seen but not noticed as we boarded the night before. I remember thinking that he must have been back with the royal children and all their servants when the lights began to flicker. I noticed that he had not had a chance to shave, so that his beard was making his pale-dark skin blue.

Then all the cattle prods went off at once, and it was like a Mickey Mouse cartoon of twenty cops disappearing into one telephone pole in a flash of precise marching. Whoosh and the young man disappeared.

Nobody faltered or blinked, and we went on walking toward the desks on our right, and the man ahead of me was escorted courteously away and then I was pulled gently out and away and I am sure the people behind me were too, but I shall never know, and I do not care.

I was led to a small white room, and a short trim woman gave

me a nice uncompromising neat smile and told me her name and
said that here she was called a lady bobby, a policewoman. Then
she apologized to me for what she had to do, and suddenly I was
about six years old again and I had to undress as fast as I could so
that it would not take long and everything would be all right and
it was nothing but a bore and would soon be over. She called me
"madam" without smiling.

The odd thing was that all the time I felt almost complacently
young and obedient, I was really being the lady bobby too, and
was feeling sorry and embarrassed and almost apologetic for her.
She was about my age, probably, and much smaller. She kept
murmuring, "Oh dear, oh dear me, how you must hate all this,
madam. Oh, what a bore! Forgive me, will you? Oh Lord."

I had never been strip-searched before, but I felt helpless and
docile, and I really liked this small neat woman. She was as sweet
as lavender, as clean as a fine razor, and I did not feel affronted in
any way at all as she pulled on rubber gloves quick as scat and
stuck one little finger up my anus and then probed all and every
orifice. It was her sweet steady little murmur that kept me from
any affront: "Oh, poor dear! This is such a bore! Over soon now,
soon, madam!"

She laughed shortly, like a puppy barking, and stood back,
pulling off the gloves. "Out! I'll come with you. Out you go, love.
Get into your things."

As she walked ahead of me, after she had helped me get back
into my clothes, I felt I wanted to see her again, to talk with her
and thank her for keeping me so dignified and for being such a
mysteriously detached, kind person. I felt that I *must* see her again.
I must thank her. But the line seemed the same, and finally I was
back on the plane, and the next time I left it was in California.

And tonight I remembered that yes, I have been body-
searched, stripped to the buff, with a gloved living probe pushed

into my secret hollows. And suddenly I remembered that at one point I asked my lady bobby in a mild, almost dreamy way, "Couldn't they do this with the cattle prods, if they are looking for whatever they found on that man?" And she said, "No, madam," and went right on.

That is all there is to report, I think, about my own small experience with this kind of police interference or whatever it may be deemed. I was fortunate in many ways. For one thing, I knew that something was very wrong with the flight I was on, whether it was mechanical or purely a problem of international politics. I felt fatalistic about it, just as I had about being put on it when I had so firmly insisted on almost any other type of flying boat, *vache-qui-vole* . . . And then I also knew that the small trim impersonal policewoman who had to look into me for hidden weapons or whatever she was told to find was one of the nicest people I had ever known.

—Glen Ellen, California, 1972

12

M. F. K. F.

*You can't accept people who fall for you.
If they fall for you, you think there's
something wrong with them.*

When I was young, I liked to reduce my schoolmates (always female) to a state of abject devotion. Then I would despise them and behave with callous arrogance and a kind of tipsy power. Instead of hating me, they seemed to like my treatment and often became longtime friends.

Gradually I saw that I felt scornful of their devotion because I knew that I was not worth loving. This proved that they were fools. So I could treat them as such . . . or as clowns, or courtiers, or plain idiots. It was cruel of me, and both sadistic and masochistic.

Later in life I did the same thing to many men. I now feel ashamed of this, as I do of mistreating my young mesdemoiselles; it seems arrogant, but actually it may have sprung from deep humility, a feeling of unworthiness. I felt that I was cheating people by letting them think that I was bright or pretty or desirable. I felt like a humbug.

And so I hated them for not seeing through me, and in turn hating me.

I don't know about all the little girls, and the adolescents, but I like to think that some of the men did see through to this truth and did hate me. They would have hated me because I had let them believe in a lie.

And this is why I am very careful about letting people like me now, although I really do feel better when I do not sense active suspicion or envy or scorn in anyone. It surprises me that I even care. But the real enjoyment of another human being is a fairly facile and sociable and usually trivial élan that one can spread. I pay almost no attention to it in gatherings where I meet many new people, but I am very cautious about using it in small groups. I do not want to *mislead* anyone.

(This is complicated to discuss, I find.)

I never hoodwinked Dillwyn, and therefore I never felt ashamed with him because I had not been anything but trusting and naive. With my first husband, Al Fisher, I think it was a mutual game we played; I loved all his tricks until I began to know that we must part, and by then neither of us really cared, although it was a cruel thing that I could not even offer him my old tempting promises. Certainly I never treated him with anything but passionate gratitude for rescuing me from the Ranch. We were mutually generous, at least on that score.

As for my third and last husband, he hated me from the first, because really he feared and loathed all women, but with him I began to despise his "use" of me as a potentially profitable literary property. He mocked my provincial habits and manners, but at the same time he bowed to my ingrown and toplofty mannerisms, left over from the early days with my very young peers. He was impressed by my faked skill at commanding the full attention of a headwaiter in a famous restaurant (simply to reduce him to furious impotence), while at the same time he sneered at my small-town mind, and hated me for bringing off what he felt was a social coup and what I myself knew was just another *trick*.

And so that went.

And now all I feel is a kind of helpless remorse at how I've been such a hoax to so many loving people, when I disliked or hated them for liking or even loving me. It is a shame, a pity.

It was not their fault but mine.

Meanwhile, this late, I accept whatever they offered me, and by now I think I know the value of what I so scornfully pushed aside when I was less aware of meanings.

The cold fact remains that I did indeed feel that people who loved me were blind and stupid to do so, instead of seeing that I was not worth the effort. And yet they did love me, and now, so late, I am grateful.

—Glen Ellen, California, 1975

13

Stealing

Sometimes stealing, or thieving, is wrong. (This means that *I* do not think it is *right*.) For instance, I don't think that Elgin should have removed the marbles to England from where he found them. Of course, they would have died, probably, if he had not. But he should have said something like "Do you mind if I move these artifacts to a relatively dry safe place where they can be preserved for our future enjoyment?"

I was raised on Gayley's *Classic Myths* (which means that I know all of the ins and outs of gods and goddesses), and I think I know about many of the intricacies of those "Elgin marbles." They were a kind of comic strip, a Mickey Mouse or Spirou story, running across the page and full of promise and threat and portent. But their removal was, to any young and now old view, a theft.

And like many others, that theft was in some way justified. Sometimes stealing is fully right.

It is my basically puritanical or moral nature that frowns on stealing, yet still leaves me feeling as innocent as anything newborn about two or three real robberies I have committed. I think I was right, just as Elgin may have been, although I reaped lesser goods.

A few minutes ago I reached for the scissors on my desk, to cut off some extra tape on a package I was wrapping, and I almost purred with pleasure to pick up *those* scissors, and feel their sure small blades cut with such pure balanced exactitude across the gummed paper. I looked at them with a small smile. They are of a dull pewterish alloy, probably, not to be polished but graceful in the hand and light to hold. They cut with a quick sureness. I would hesitate to take them to a sharpener in this country; he might try to brighten the look of them, or put the slim blades under the electric sharpener.

I decided to steal them about three hours after I moved into a rented apartment in southern France. It was the bottom floor of a *mas* or farm, owned by an architect in Paris/London. I did not know her, and of course hope I never meet her because of my thievery, but she was a friend of a friend, and she let me stay there for several weeks. When I finally left for other pastures, I took the/ *my* scissors without a thought, because they had been mine since the minute I saw them in the top right-hand drawer under the kitchen sink. I moved them at once into the other room and put them on a table that would be my desk, and from then until this minute, many years later, I feel good when I see their almost dainty shape and their subtle color, and I feel thankful that I took them with me. (That is a euphemism: I *stole* them.)

I left three pairs of good metal, more modern of course, in their place; in the kitchen and on the desk and another in a closet. They cost plenty, but the pair I stole was, and I admitted it, *irreplaceable*.

I think—in fact, I feel sure—that the architect never knew

that my scissors were gone. I have never written to inquire. I could
—but why?

Of course if I'd stolen a baby, or a fine painting, I'd write and
say why I did so. I might even be jailed or hung, even if the stolen
goods were not wanted or were never looked at.

But my scissors are wanted (coveted, desired), and I look at
them several times a week with an inner delight at their delicate
precision.

Of course I've stolen one or two other things in my life. I
suppose that most people have, if they look back far enough to
admit sin at all.

Once I did not steal, and I shall always be sorry, and repelled
by my cowardice. I was staying with friends in a rented house in a
canyon in Hollywood. There were a lot of ugly steps going up to
the really ugly house at the top. My husband and I were tutoring
the children of O. K., a refugee conductor from Berlin. He was
renting the house from a film writer, so that there were a lot of
books, mostly French, which I read while the scared kids learned
to breathe again and in another language. And there was one book
I decided to steal, at the end of that strange summer of *mittagessen*
[midday meals] and famous Americans and having to sit in the
conductor's box at the Hollywood Bowl.

It was a book I read, by an Englishman named Cyril Something, I think, that had about three pages of superb and unforgettable prose in it. It was about a baseball game. I had never been to
one. It described a game played outdoors in crystal light, with tiny
athletes, tiny watchers, darling tiny lights and colors and faces and
figures and bodies in the clear light. He told all that about a
baseball game. And I knew I had to take that book.

I did not want to embarrass the friends we were living with
while we had the job with the conductor's children, but as the
summer ended slowly (because I felt so sad for the children trying

to be in a new world—the father seemed beyond human pity by then, and I never really saw the opera-singer mother except as a gracious bowing female at the Bowl), I began to plan ways to get the book.

It seems odd now (and suddenly I remember a name: Cyril Hume—I must investigate) that I did not talk or ask or tell that I wanted that one book because of that one beautiful description.

I had seen and felt the light the author described, a few years earlier—it was like being in a country fair by Brueghel. My father and I had gone up to Whittier College from the Ranch so that he could report on a town gathering: he was editor of the *News* in Whittier. We went out onto the football field, at near twilight, and there in a crystalline and impeccable beauty were townspeople, known but transmogrified, moving like angels on earth in a green delicate electric beauty. I remember it now as I write about it, and I feel breathless. It was a moment caught in time, like a fly in amber, maybe. The light went from the west and the Pacific over toward the eastern hills, and then from the flat grasslands to the mountains and the Salton Sea. It slanted all the shadows eastward. The familiar football field was packed with ambling happy people eating almost languidly from long tables, and talking, smiling, moving in the magic.

I have never seen that again, anywhere. But the book captured it, and I don't remember if it was at an American college or where. But it was the magical way of catching the light that was there in that cheap ignored book, which I felt I must steal.

I did not. We all left the house, a drab elegant sad place that one day later was sold. I asked vaguely, several months after, what had happened to the books and was told that someone had bought all of them by shelf, at five dollars a foot or something like that.

So there went that book I knew I should steal.

But whom would I have asked? The owner of the house was

not there. Our host was gone most of the time. So was my husband, who could not have told me to take the book anyway. And I was pusillanimous.

About a year later, I was going down Hollywood Boulevard and saw a tall white-haired heavily shaded man weaving, staggering in a nice well-behaved way, and it was, I was told, the once-famous or well-known English writer who had "come to Hollywood."

I felt badly, and I still do. I wish I had got out and gone over to the old lush—or perhaps he was not much older than I—and told him that he had written. in *My Sister My Birds,* one of my own dreams.

—Glen Ellen, California, 1976

14

Fossils

Out of the nowhere and into the here (Where did you come from, baby dear?) a cloud drifts swiftly through and over, and I wonder what I ate for breakfast or lunch, a few thousand light miles away in my inconsequence. What did I really do since I last came into consciousness at about 5:45 this morning? Did I pot a hybrid tomato? Was I really at the lunch table with two strangers passing through the Valley of the Moon? They had called two days before, and I had made a nice little meal for us, with some good wine . . .

But where was I? Am I asking this of Time, or Space?

The only reassurance I can give myself in this spinning world is to look at and even to think about older things than I, and to laugh at my ephemeral state. I have several such reminders of it. Of course, there are furniture, silver, pictures, all that, but they are almost as transitory as I. The best things are the fossils.

I saw one in a window a couple of years ago. In fact, I saw

two, and so did my younger sister, and neither of us could afford to buy them, but we kept looking in as we went through the Passage Agard in Aix, and thinking about them in our own ways. They were small exquisite imprints or skeletons, or whatever archaeologists call them, of little fish, about two inches long, and slanted sideways into aluminum cases designed by their finder in the southern French terrain. He was an engineer, we were told, who had forgotten everything but the pursuit of the tiny fish, thirty million years old, which he caught in his strange metallic showcases. We kept looking at them, and the day before we had to leave that fair country again I left my sister and went up the Passage and bought the two fish, so long imprisoned. She had one, and I had one, and we felt fine about it.

Once back in California, I showed mine to a friend who goes on erudite diggings and half starves and has diarrhea but feels renewed inwardly by finding that this planet was lived on long before we evolved. She found my tiny old fish pretty enough, but the next time she came she gave me a beautiful lump that was obviously a clam shell molded around solid lava or prehistoric clay, and it was not thirty million years old but one hundred and fifty million.

I held it gently, although I think I could have bounced it off the floor, and I agreed that she had topped my joke. And now I look at it and think of it, although I look oftener at the less clumpy and much younger fish that the ex-engineer found and shaved and mounted for me in the southern mountains of France.

There are many less ancient but equally matured things around me, and I find some reassurance in them, or at least amusement. Now and then I wonder why I like oldness. It is certainly not a question of my own age, since from my first conscious days I have known and sought out and wooed older men and women. The main trouble with this fixation or habit or whatever it may be called is that in the end one is left forsaken, since men usually die younger than women and even an eighty-year-old female will die sooner than one twenty years her junior. This is an emotional hazard that must be faced, and owning a fossilized tiny fish or a clunky old clam shell makes it seem more reasonable.

—*Glen Ellen, California, 1976*

15

Empty Cupboards

Once I spent several weeks as a professional guest of a famous teacher of gastronomy from America. We were in the far south of France, in the house of another famous teacher of gastronomy from America. I got to the somewhat isolated country house about midmorning, under my own steam because my host and his wife had to be away. I was very hungry, indeed almost famished. But I felt secure in this epicurean stronghold, and once I had emptied a few things like hairpins and slippers into the sumptuous quarters obviously meant for me, I headed for the kitchen of the silent house. I felt a little desperate for food after the long train ride and a night in a hotel dedicated at that time of the year to overfed tourists from Luxembourg. I went first to the icebox in the good dim cool kitchen, which was Americanized but still real, with a scoured and generous table in the middle. I felt fine and at home in that kitchen. But the icebox was empty, except for one withered small tomato at the bottom. I doubt that I have ever seen such an empty icebox: there was no cheese in the pullout metal compartment labeled CHEESE, and there was nothing in EGGS, and except for the dead tomato there was nothing in RE-FRESHER. Certainly there was nothing in MEATS. And since this humming little machine was something of an astonishment in that neighborhood, there was no kind of freezer. It was enough to survive as a plain icebox in southern France!

I went impatiently to the shelves that lined the good room promisingly, but all I turned up was a strangely shaped tin mentioning duck packed in cabbage. I must admit, this far from the scene, that I seized on it and then looked vainly, in every one of the many drawers, for a way to open it. If I could have, I think I would have gnawed the whole little duck to its marrow. As it was, I felt like tearing into the tin with my teeth, except that I recognized their merits. There was nothing for me to do but contain myself and contemplate my navel, which I did.

This pecular introduction to a transplanted American kitchen cult gave me great pause to wonder, and I have thought long and often about it. There we were, my hosts and I, in a land almost audibly bursting with delicious vegetables springing from the soil. In the village up the hill were three or four places where farmers left their culls as they went to the markets in Cannes and Nice and Grasse: boxes and baskets filled with small ripe tomatoes, green beans as slender as knitting needles, dirty scraggly lettuces with hearts as sweet as milk, little tennis balls of zucchini, olives of every color, and now and then a few late but still tender almonds in their green coats. There were not many fruits then, except for melons and some cherries from the high meadows, but the wasps still came to taste in front of the main store, and inside there was a simple supply of cheese and, twice a week, some of the best plain bread I have ever eaten. I came to know all this because I stayed hungry all the time I lived with the famous teacher of gastronomy, for there was never anything more than I had first found in his icebox. He went out. I did too, when it seemed best for professional reasons. Otherwise I subsisted on little sneaky snacks. I even hired a taxi a few times and went to Grasse, where I headed for an open-front stand where a man or a girl made huge paper-thin pancakes on a stove on the sidewalk. I would eat one folded over with cheese. Then I would eat one made with ham. Then, to the astonishment of the man and the girl and perhaps the other customers, I would eat one made with sugar and lemon juice. And under my legs at the table (there were three small ones, behind the griddle) would be a few things I hoped we could perhaps eat in the beautiful kitchen, instead of going out to another two-star restaurant screaming with tourists from Luxembourg (the richer ones). We never did, and the few things I bought at first, like green almonds and small pungent olives and slices of peculiar sausages, gradually diminished; I knew that unless I ate all of them myself they would die. Finally, once, in an almost adolescent rage at this gastronomical impasse and deception, I bought a bar of chocolate. I put it on the nightstand in my lovely room, and a couple of days later I threw it, unwrapped, into a thicket of surging herbs and wildflowers under an olive tree.

—Glen Ellen, California, 1977

16

Thimble

There is a difference between owning and possessing.

I am thinking now of my thimble, strangely enough for me because I never much liked to sew, although at times I have done it well. Sewing has always served as a practical rather than an aesthetic means to an end. In contrast, my goddaughter Solveig is an unpaid designer and executer of beautiful patchwork. But I have never done more than darn stockings when I had to, patch pillow slips to save them, make dresses if I could not buy them.

This morning I was tidying my household sewing kit, and I found more than six thimbles. Among them was an oddly familiar one of darkish steel with a wide band of rather boring gold around it. It looked a little Pre-Raphaelite, and it must have been designed in perhaps 1900, because on one section of the tiny mixture, written up and down and romantic, there are my mother's initials—four, because she was married in 1904. I must send it to Solveig in Wiltshire, I thought.

And I thought about one time when I was between eight and eleven and I felt that my grandmother's thimble must sometime belong to me. I did not crave to own it. I am sure there was no overt lust. Neither did I want to *have* it. I simply assumed that it should and would be mine.

It was made of gold, and very finely, and because my grandmother was a Puritan who believed and practiced abstinence from all physical pleasures, it surprises me that she permitted herself to use this gaudy elegance. For it was set around the bottom with perhaps six glowing buttons of coral, softly orange-pink, and above them, before the little indentations to catch the needle tips, common to all thimbles, there was an exquisite engraving, all around the thimble, of a *village!* There was a church as the focal point, of course, and along one side of the main street stood tiny cottages and even a shop or two near the church. It was almost invisible except to a child's eye, complete there between the coral and the grainy golden tip of Grandmother's thimble, and I looked at it with what I now think was complacency but even then accepted as true pleasure. It would be in my care, I knew.

As I looked at it in the sewing basket or on my grandmother's finger, I loved knowing that my own eye had seen the church and the shops and the cottages strung out for perhaps half a mile above the smooth beads of pink stone and that Grandmother had let me use her name and later would lend me her thimble. She first taught me how to knit and then purl, so that in 1917 I made a little pale green pullover, big enough for a young baby perhaps, that was auctioned at the first public Red Cross meeting after "we" entered World War I, which my family had been quietly fighting since 1914 because of our connections in Europe. My contribution cost some patriot seven dollars, I was told somewhat deprecatingly the next day.

I felt at least seven inches taller, until Grandmother said coldly that perhaps I was now qualified to try knitting a stocking. Still, I felt more elated then deflated, because the little pullover, while only a step higher than the straight knit mufflers I had been knitting in hideous khaki-colored yarn for Our Boys in Britain, was still infinitely better than Mother's Washrag, as we all called it.

Edith, whose thimble reminded me of this when it turned up this morning in my spring cleaning, hated to sew, knit, clean, cook, in fact, do anything her mother expected her to do. That is doubtless why her thimble is still so fresh and dainty. She tried *not* to use it properly, so that all her seams pulled out and all her hems fell. And while all of us sat furiously knitting mufflers and mittens and scarves for Our Boys and turning out tiny masterpieces for the Red Cross, Mother worked with scant amusement, throughout the whole war, on a washrag of gradually graying wool that she kept laughing about as she deliberately dropped stitches and forgot whether to purl three or knit two. It was a small family joke, and only Grandmother, who did very much resemble Queen Victoria in her general grim small plumpness, was "not amused."

I, with one eye on my clumsy smiling mother and the other on my stern grandam, sat much of the day with the elder, who was always kind, if imposing, and I learned a lot about many ways to read the Bible and at the same time sew a strong seam. I agreed when Grandmother told me that a lady's hands are never idle. And all the time, as I learned almost unwittingly to sew and read and knit and stay silent until spoken to, I was watching Grandmother's beautiful thimble.

Of course she did not wear it except for sewing, but as I try to remember how she sat in a low chair in the sunroom with me leaning against her knees and the two of us keeping an eye on the new little sister lying on an afghan in the soft warm light, I think that the more I was learning to knit, the more she was sewing, mending all our tears and snags, making clothes for the next baby, doing cross-stitch samplers for me to try to copy.

Her daughter Edith best liked to keep her idle hands free to hold up a novel, any novel but mostly English, as she lay undoubtedly working out our procreative schedule. Perhaps this is why it never entered my young mind that I would ever use her thimble, the one with the late William Morris look in its gold band.

And it never occurred to me that the oddly luxurious and elegant thimble that Grandmother used daily, as if it were a cheap steel-tin job, would not one day be mine. After all, she and I had the same names—Mary Frances—and she had taught me to read, which I still do, although not with my mother's abandonment of several other pleasures.

But when I was about eleven, a plump dull cousin turned up for the summer, as many relatives did in those preplane days of more frequent and longer visits, and one day Grandmother said to her, "Here, this thimble is for you, my dear," and the cousin put it in her pocket and probably lost it on the long way home without even knowing she had what was really mine.

And that is why I know there is a difference between owning and possessing.

—*Glen Ellen, California, 1978*

17

Not Enough

Perhaps the main difference between Norah and me is that while we are friends (by now), she still thinks of me as her older sister, and I think of her mostly as a friend.

Or in other words, I ask for and accept many things from her that she has never asked from me. I have often called on her for help, and she has without hesitation changed all her complicated plans and come as fast as possible, and I have never doubted her love or her familial devotion. But she is a prouder person than I am, and as yet she has seldom admitted to purely human weaknesses, although lately she does creak audibly when the going is rough.

Once, though, when she asked me for immediate loving help, I stood her off. I think now and then of this strange happening, with self-disgust, or at least an uncomfortable kind of self-doubt.

One Sunday at the Ranch, in perhaps 1950, I asked Nan and Chuck Newton and their little boy Chas to come for lunch, mostly to perk up Rex a little but also because I enjoyed them very much and my girls loved Chas. Rex ambled out in his Sunday velvet house jacket, plainly old and grumpy and not well, and when Chuck came they went off in a corner and Nan came out to help me get lunch, and the children were on the side porch on the floor, playing something.

Norah telephoned from Los Angeles, I think, and she said that she was up there from Sunset Beach where she was living while she and John got a divorce, and that she had a badly infected thumb or finger and that John would drive her and the three children out to the Ranch instead of her going back down to the beach. I said OK, fine indeed. And sorry about the hand. And she said they'd be there in an hour.

So Nan and I held off lunch, and we told Rex that we were going to wait for Norah and the boys, and he suddenly became almost hysterical and was very bitter about John Barr: he'd never set foot on the Ranch again, by God, and so on. I was a treacherous female to let him weasel back in this way, etc., etc.

Chuck took care of him, and Nan and I half fed the three little kids and then we waited around, and finally the car drove in, and Rex got very upset again and Chuck calmed him again, and Nan and I went into the kitchen to welcome the poor lost roaming Barrs.

The two older boys, very small and quick, dashed in and at once settled themselves onto the floor with Chas and my girls, and I think John brought Matt to the door, the back porch door.

Norah came last, looking very gaunt and wan, with one heavily bandaged hand held up as she'd been told to do, after minor but nasty surgery to lance an infection. She was shot full of whatever one was given in those far days—penicillin? She sailed in, and Nan came out to get Matt, and I said to John that Rex was on a tear and would not let him come in.

It was a bad moment.

I think John trusted me as much as he could any of us in those hard days, and he unloaded some stuff from Norah's car so that she could stay overnight with the three boys instead of going down to the beach—the doctors had prescribed several days of rest, but how can a single woman with three small children tackle that?—and then he got into my car and we drove almost silently up to the bus station. We gave each other a good friendly hug, and I did not see him again for several years, which was all right.

When I got back, Norah was standing in the dining room, beautiful and disdainful. Behind her through the three wide-open French doors sat the five little children, aware of tensions and thunder but playing on the floor, something about cards and dice. Nan and Chuck sat having a drink with Rex in the dim living room.

Norah suddenly put both arms around me as if to hold me with passion, a most unfamiliar gesture in our overly decorous family. She was vibrating the way a good arrow vibrates or thrums or shivers after it has been shot out and has then plunged into its target.

But instead of bending to her need for aid and succor, I did what still haunts me (thank God, rarely), and I stiffened and gently undid her long loving needing arms from my shoulders.

She was whimpering. I looked down over her high shoulder and saw the worried eyes of five little children looking with pain and puzzlement up at our sadness, and I said, as I pulled off her beseeching arms, "The children are looking. Stop this!"

I do not know how I said this short cruel thing, but I believe that I was trying to protect them all, no matter how foolishly, from something I myself feared—our futures, maybe.

Norah stiffened and withdrew, and I knew that I had lost a moment of need and comfort that would never happen again. She looked down at the five little mice peering up at us and said with so strong a scorn that it was almost shocking, "To hell with them."

It was a flat statement. The children paled with shock, and then as I withdrew from Norah's desperate embrace, their faces calmed and they went on with whatever it was they were playing —cards, bones . . .

We went into the living room and behaved properly and then went back to the dining room and behaved properly, and after a long good winey lunch, Nan and I tended to the kitchen stuff and Norah, who was saggy-dizzy with past pain and present medical stress, sat on a tuffet while Chuck played old Fats Waller records in a dim corner of the living room. Rex sat at the other end, smoking.

Nobody seemed to know but me and perhaps Norah—who may by now have forgotten it, if she ever realized it—that I had rejected her that day. Why did I say "the children"? She was right, in the long run, to say, "To hell with them." She needed *me* then, and I was not ready to forget the demands of my current world and give her the true warm love I shall always feel for her.

—*Glen Ellen, California, 1978*

 18

Then

By 9:59 P.M., the crescent moon and the satellite had set beyond the Jack London ridges to the west. A fine sight.

I sat in deep silence, and I was in Laguna—Arch Rock, Top of the World. The time was important. The place was chooseable there, depending on temperature and local whims. Here the place seems set. And time is even less out of control than when Aunt Gwen would say mildly in the morning that we'd watch the sun set from this or that rock, cliff, hill along the coast.

—*Glen Ellen, California, 1978*

19

Interviews—I

I've often said that I'm proud of being a fifth-generation newspaper person, and indeed I am. I feel that real newspaper people, on any level of the pecking order, can be and more often than not *are* honest human beings of integrity and scruples.

Many of my friends love to tease me about the horrible lack of both scruples and honesty in many good journalists, who print gossip for political reasons, who deliberately misquote, who take things out of context, and all that business. This is true, I know. But in general I admire and like newspaper people.

However, I feel very strongly about one thing in modern journalism, and that is the use of long, close-knit, often photographed interviews, which are run exactly as is a one-inch squib at the bottom of page six. They are never read back to the subjects. More often than not it is the so-called editorial policy not to check in any way on fairly important but not essential-to-the-minute interviews with people like me, or with much more important people in every field. A feature writer, and usually a photographer or a sound man who tapes the whole thing, will spend a day or two on a story, and then the writer is never allowed to check back or even to read it by telephone to the interviewee. Of course, one common complaint is that some of the people interviewed want to rewrite the articles. I would never think of doing that, but I do think that the vital facts, for instance, should be checked, even double-checked.

In one year, I remember, I was born in Atlanta, Georgia, and Nome, Alaska, and I was said to be peaking sixty and well into my eighties (I was really about seventy, I think). So I feel, and very strongly, that editorially there is a difference between a feature story on a person and a straight news story.

One time I was asked to give a long interview to a young woman I know in San Francisco. She was trying to be a feature writer for a local newspaper, and she suggested that she do a story on my recent trip to Japan. She came here with three other people: a sound woman and maybe two photographers. She wanted to talk about a book I'd worked on with a Japanese friend.

I'd had a rather boring time with that book, because I was expected and even believed to be an erudite, rather sententious writer, very scholastic—in sum, *well educated.* Instead, I'd written a rather light, informal, almost flippant introduction to the very formal subject of classical Japanese cooking.

The newspaper people and I talked very seriously all morning and everything I said was recorded. Then, I remember, we all sat down to a nice long lunch. We chatted about personal things: the girl's absent husband, some mutual friends. I said once, "This is all off the air, isn't it?" She said, "Of course."

We talked on, informally, about how I was trying very hard to have the newspaper guild acknowledge that there is a difference between "in-depth" interviews and short squibs of local or newsworthy interest that are run immediately, so that there is no time to check anything. The girl said very firmly that she could not possibly go against the paper's policy of never checking back. We left it at that.

Then, about two hours after the story came out, which I suppose was within the next week, the Japanese consul general in San Francisco called me personally to ask me *why* or *if* I had said, for a local paper, that our walls and our car and our bathroom were bugged all the time I was in Japan with my sister.

I was horrified, and he was very cold, and I didn't blame him one bit. Indeed I had said just that, and it was true.

I felt quite sure then, and I do still feel sure, that we were bugged, but it was not particularly important. It did not bother us a bit. We didn't ever say anything that we shouldn't have said. "God, a drink would taste good! . . . Hurry up! . . . Should I wear the pants or the skirt?" And was it my sister's turn to go to the bathroom? What we said was of no political or social importance at all, but it was checked, and probably rightfully so, because we were being treated almost imperially by the Japanese government, as well as by our hosts. And I could not blame the consul general for being irate and upset at what sounded like a betrayal of national courtesy.

I was furious with the young reporter, because she had printed something that had nothing to do in any possible way with the story she got from me. It was a piece of non sequitur chitcat, dropped into her report without any reason at all. Furthermore, she heard me say it after we had sat down at the table and were talking informally and off the record. I thought this was a breach not only of manners and etiquette but of professional decency. I felt sick about it then, and I still do.

There was one other time when I felt rather sick about bad newspaper manners. A California magazine that was published in

San Francisco and Los Angeles called me in Sonoma. The editor was out of town, but his secretary asked me if I could give her a quick little thing that would run with items on a group of about ten writers who were being interviewed. Of course I agreed. It was an easy favor.

The question we were each asked was, What would you do with a very famous stranger if he came suddenly for one day? Where would you entertain him, and how? I asked if anything I said would be read back to me before the magazine went to press. The girl said, "Of course, of *course!*" Then she named Craig Claiborne as the man who would be thrust upon me for one day.

The funny thing was that right across from me at my lunch table sat Craig, who was an old friend and a good one. We grinned at each other, and I went on talking on the telephone. I felt hysterically amused by this situation, and I said solemnly among other things that Mr. Claiborne had to go out a lot. She said, "Where would you go to dinner? *How* would you take a famous man like that to dinner?" We were eating a very nice lunch at that moment, but he was going to stay for supper too, so I said, "Well, probably a man like Mr. Claiborne would be invited out so much to restaurants that I think it would be rather nice to ask him just to come to my house." Then I added, "After all, there are no really exciting places here in town to go to, anyway!"

Well, of course, I never would have said that last at all, if I had been writing it, or talking less hastily. And I assumed that I would have it read back to me, when I would have caught it at once, and deleted it. But I didn't think, and the girl didn't call me back, and I forgot the whole silly incident.

Then, about two weeks later, after the appearance of the little magazine, the telephone rang, and it was a local restaurateur, a friend of mine. He was almost crying. At first he sounded abjectly hurt, and he said among other things, "You've driven the last nail in my coffin," because he was having a rather hard time financially. Then he got quite abusive, and it was very unpleasant indeed.

I immediately wrote to the editor of the local paper and told him I was in a pickle. What should I do? What he did was to print my letter as a kind of a statement of my deep regret, and of why I had done such a thing, and of how I had fully expected my words to be deleted if I'd had the chance to hear the story before it went to press.

I also wrote a coolish letter to the magazine editor. I didn't want to get his secretary into trouble, but it was a very careless thing for her to do, I thought, not to call me, not even to tell him. He was upset, too. (She was not fired.)

I feel very badly about how this silly bit of journalistic carelessness has changed my whole feeling about going to my friend's restaurant. He has been hurt, and I hate that!

I think these are my two newspaper gaffes that I know about, but I am very sure I have said or done other things that have seemed rude or crude or indiscreet, in some way or other.

I remember one thing I did *not* say that caused a little pain. Many years ago I came home to Whittier after a long time away. I was making my living then as a freelance magazine writer, mostly about food, and I'd said something, laughingly, about how people in small-town tearooms (there were lots of tearooms in the thirties and forties) always brought around trays of relishes and little baskets of hot bread, buns, muffins. The patrons nibbled away, and the more generous and lavish the trays of homemade relishes and hot rolls were, the more they thought they were eating a generous lot of free food, which of course they weren't. I wrote something about that, not mocking or supercilious, but pleasantly teasing.

Then, when I got home, my mother was almost tearful about how hurtful I had been to the local tearoom people! She and

Father went there about twice a week, when it was the cook's night off. Often they took my sisters Norah or Anne. It was a very nice tearoom. It was in what had been the living room of a house. The waitresses were inept but nice young schoolgirls, friends of the granddaughter of the woman who ran it, etc. It was *nice*. There were creaky floors, I suppose, no rugs . . .

This was about the time when people put candles in bottles and let the wax run down, and felt rather bohemian. And they did indeed have these candles at this tearoom, which was called something like the Grape Arbor or the Rose Trellis. They did indeed have trays of relishes, and they did indeed serve the owner's famous hot muffins with raisins in them.

I'd never been there in my life, and of course I was not laughing at it, but Mother said that the people, all of them fellow church members, now hardly spoke to her, and that she didn't dare set her foot in there, because I had been so cruel about them. I felt awful . . . but it was funny too, in a way, and later everything was all right.

This was an inadvertent slip of my own journalistic manners, I suppose. But the other two were careless errors and really not my fault. It is hard to earn your living as a writer, or even as a freelance hack, and always think of how every word will look in print to every single person who reads it. I have never done that, and I never can—nor will I, nor should I. But it is dreadful to have a good man cry over the phone, and tell you that you've driven the last nail in his coffin. That's *bad*.

I think I am going to fight as long as I live, through authors' leagues and newspaper guilds and also by word of mouth and so on, to get the editorial people to separate plain news from interviews. There is no reason why any editor who has time and money enough to send out a feature writer and a photographer from New York cannot afford to have his writer pick up the phone and check on when and where I was born. This would be a courteous and face-saving thing to do, and it would strengthen my unfaltering if occasionally battered faith in the basic decency of the newspaper profession.

—Glen Ellen, California, 1979

20

Poor Food

I am thinking now of some of the best meals in my life, and almost without exception they have been so because of the superlative honesty of "poor food," rather than sophistication. I admire and often even *like* what is now called the classical cuisine —the intricate sauces of great chefs, and the complexities of their entremets and their pastries. But for strength, both of the body and of the spirit, I turn without hesitation to the simplest cooks.

I remember the best sauce I ever ate.

It was not at Foyot's, in the old days in Paris. It was in a cabin with tar-paper walls on a rain-swept hillside in southern California. The air was heavy with the scent of wet sage from outside and the fumes of a cheap kerosene stove within. Three or four children piped for more, more, from the big bowl of steaming gravy in the center of the heavy old round table crowded between the family's cots. We ate it from soup plates, the kind you used to get free with labels from cereal packages. It was made from a couple of young cottontails, and a few pulls of fresh herbs from the underbrush, and springwater and some Red Ink from the bottom of Uncle Johnnie's birthday jug—and a great deal of love. It was all we had, with cold flapjacks left from breakfast to scoop it up. It was *good,* and I knew that I was indeed fortunate, to have driven up the hill that night in the rain and to have friends who would share with me.

I remember the best stew I ever ate, too.

It was not a bouillabaisse at Isnard's in Marseille. It was made, further east on the Mediterranean at Cassis, by a very old small woman for a great lusty batch of relatives and other people she loved. Little grandnephews dove for equally young octopuses and delicate sea eggs, and older sons sent their rowboats silently up the dark *calanques* for rockfish lurking among the sunken German U-boats from the First War, and grizzling cousins brought in from the deep sea a fine catch of rays and other curious scaly monsters. Little girls and their mothers and great-aunts went up into the bone-dry hills for aromatic leaves and blossoms, and on the way home picked up a few bottles of herby wine from the tiny vineyards where they worked in the right seasons.

The very old small woman cooked and pounded and skinned and ruminated, and about noon, two days later, we met in her one-room house and spent some twenty more hours, as I remember, eating and eating . . . and talking and singing and then eating again, from seemingly bottomless pots of the most delicious stew in my whole life. It, again, had been made with love . . .

And out of a beautiful odorous collection of good breads in my life I still taste, in my memory, the *best.*

There have been others that smelled better, or looked better, or cut better, but this one, made by a desolately lonesome Spanish-Greek Jewess for me when I was about five, was the best. Perhaps it was the shape. It was baked in pans just like the big ones we used every Saturday, but tiny, perhaps one by three inches. And it rose just the way ours did, but tinily. (Many years later, when I read *Memoirs of a Midget* and suffered for the difficulties of such a small person's meals, I wished I could have taken to her, from time to time and wrapped in a doll's linen napkin, a fresh loaf from my friend's oven.)

Yes, that was and still is the best bread. It came from the kitchen of a very simple woman, who knew instinctively that she could solace her loneliness through the ritual of honest cooking. It taught me, although I did not understand it then, a prime lesson in survival. I must eat well. And in these days of spurious and distorted values, the best way to eat is simply, without affectation or adulteration. Given honest flour, pure water, and a good fire, there is really only one more thing needed to make the best bread in the world, fit for the greatest gourmet ever born: and that is honest love.

—Glen Ellen, California, 1979

21

Noëls Provençaux

The problem: should I try to carve a smoked trout for lunch tomorrow for a Ticinese patrician and her Philadelphia lover or write about what these strange piping songs have done? I resolve everything by ignoring the smoked trout.

I have been listening to a new recording of music played in Provence at Christmas. It is very neat and slick and well done, and it was made in the Abbey Saint Victor in Marseille, right below where I lived for some time. It is *echt* all right, and the acoustics in that familiar vault are right for it, but still it is not the way I hear inwardly that ancient Greek-Roman piping and drumming.

The first time it got into my blood and heart I was almost unaware of it, except as something in the dream of submissive ignorant bliss in which I lived with my first husband. We went blindly down from Dijon to the Côte d'Or in 1929; Cassis was an almost unknown fishing village then.

Germans took it over in 1940 and built a casino there for the officers, and later it was a convenient and beautiful place for both the French and foreigners, but when we went there, it was an ancient secret tiny port, dangerous to find on the Mediterranean coast between Marseille and Toulon, and with few trains that would stop up on the highlands for an occasional tourist. There were no taxis and, in winter, no restaurants. The few villagers who used the train walked up to the station and down, with a quick stop at the chapel on the way.

So the landlord of the little hotel on the quay, who had probably been tipped off about our naiveté by his old school pal and our landlord in Dijon, led us gently to the door of his inn at about 11:30 on Christmas Eve, and pointed our noses up the hill. We walked fast in the chilly air that seems right on Christmas Eve, even in Provence, and got there in time to find a place in the small redolent chapel. It was lit, as I now remember, by many tapers, and by torches outside the entrance. It was glowing and warm.

A choir sang in the little loft above our heads, with much shuffling and rustling of voices and starched vestments. Men marched in the church door blowing on wooden flutes and curved things and what I assume were oboes *(hautbois),* and there were several proud prancing young drummers beating their tambours with one hand and piping with the other. Then there was a procession of *people,* who took their places near the altar. I do not remember all I saw that night, but of course I know now that they were Joseph and Mary and that the shepherds came along and then Three Wise Men. All the time the piping and the tambours' beat and the high innocent crying of the woodwinds flickered with the candles in the little chapel, and it got into me without my knowing it.

We went out with the rest of the people, down to the little quay-side hotel, where we were given some wine and cake because we were strangers at the family feast.

That night a small furtive cargo ship docked under the windows of the hotel. I watched in silence. I put on my husband's overcoat, so that I could stand by the open window in the chill. The ship was plainly bringing in some kind of contraband, as a handful of men moved like silent rats from it into two or three dark open doors along the quay. Before dawn it slid away and out past the flickering harbor light.

It was a death ship, I knew, because I had read B. Traven's books and I recognized the horrible rattle in its doomed engines, just as I knew when and why the humans who scuttled across the quay were coughing their lives quietly into the blackness. But all the time I stood there looking down, my mind and my heart were uplifted by the sound of music I had not actually heard, so shy had I felt at being there in the glowing chapel, a stranger, and an innocent one.

By now I know a lot more about the music of Provence, if not its strange age-old traffickings. What slips in and out of small and large ports, by sea or air or even land, cannot hurt the sound of the music that still beats there in that rocky and gutty and haunted old country.

As I matured, slowly, I began to hear all the music in the pageant. I have returned there like a homing pigeon for countless years since that far-gone day—perhaps it is my "spiritual home." And the music is in my blood, from that first stupid open loving trial, in the little chapel in Cassis.

The underlying Near East sounds began gradually to hit my spirit, and by now I am astonished at how overt the acceptance is and perhaps always has been, in Provence, of this skirling whirling sensuous tantalizing rhythm from North Africa, from Algiers and Tunis and Morocco and westward.

It came easily to me to listen, once I was in Provence as an older person. And finally I lived on a street in Aix where the women left their radios turned high, all day, to broadcasts of Algerian disc jockeys. The wailing beat in, but it did not bother me, any more than the sound of pipes wailing in Provençal music can. I had heard it before, and was waiting . . .

So after that first ignorant Christmas in Cassis, with all that music in my inner heart, it took some time and space to get back to it, and even more to know what I had heard. By then the "Noëls de Provence" were becoming fashionable folklore. They were being televised. People reserved seats at high prices to fly down to Les Baux, for instance, where the helpless lamb or goat kid was still trundled in as the cameras whirred, and the society reporters caught names, and the innkeepers chilled the Dom Pérignon or other fashionable wines, and laid out fatuous dainties.

But the music was still good, even when stylish. The local people who could tootle their old cornets and oboes, and mostly the youngsters who wanted to go on playing pipes and drums, kept right on. This was heartening.

Once, not at Christmas but at Easter, a whole churchful of people in Aix waited because a young lamb being led down the street to enact the pageant was late for some reason. The music piped on, and people fidgeted, and two minor priests went out to the steps of the big doors to watch. Finally the lamb came, in the arms of his young shepherd who had missed a bus somewhere, and the mass began.

One time in Aix, my children and I bought tickets to watch the *Pastorale*, which is an enactment of the coming of Mary and Joseph to Provence. The story is that the village where they sought an inn was torn with hatred and strife. The miller could not work with the mayor. The priest was uppity. The old woman who sold fish quarreled daily with the miller. Then the Baby was born in a manger because none of these bitches and bastards had room for such a problem, and at once they all turned into sappy-happy saints. They loved one another. They lifted their hands to heaven, and rolled their eyes.

And all the time the pipers and drummers, with that strange undercurrent of Eastern enticement, played their songs. Sometimes the tunes were short and bouncy, and sometimes almost reverential and churchlike—because a short time ago, like 45 A.D., the south of France became somewhat Christianized when Mary Magdalene and some of her family and servants landed at a little port called Les Saintes Maries de la Mer.

She had been put adrift in a boat after the death of Jesus of Nazareth, who had told her she could baptize his people. She left with some relatives and hangers-on and a pot of magical chickpeas, which lasted all of them for days or weeks and became the symbol of nourishment for countless generations. She made her way to a good drippy grotto and after some thirty years died of bronchitis, and became a saint. But in spite of all that she is still a leading citizen of Provence (and especially Marseille, for various reasons connected perhaps with her early life of ease and promiscuity).

So the Oriental influence seems logical in Provençal music. It is there all the time, and in the new records I have been listening to, made in 1979 in Marseille, it is very good, if "contrived." (By that I mean that it seems cleaned up and even perfected, alongside the stuff I have listened to and lived into, in many places in Provence. It is "slick.")

I know that there is by now the whir of the sound machines in the ancient chapels, and the glare of lights and the musicians have been rehearsed and they wear makeup; and the audience will appear next week in fashionable West-World journals—but the music is still compelling, probably because it is so old/new.

Once my two daughters and I were living on the top floor of a little hotel in Aix, so that they could be near their schools. The hotel was owned by the elderly son of one of Frédéric Mistral's band, called the Félibriges. All those young men dedicated to reviving and prolonging the local language of the Languedoc met there, and the dining room of the little hotel was decorated with a delightful mural on three sides, painted on good canvas, of the old countryside between Arles and Aix, or Aix and Avignon. It was banal but irretrievably beautiful. The dining room was no longer used, but we liked to sit in there for home lessons: Latin, French history . . .

Next to our two-room palace on the fifth floor was a little cubbyhole for special favorites of our landlord, and one of these, a descendant of one of Mistral's intimates, was a boy about twenty who was a *folklorien.* He carried on the ancient art of playing his tambour with his left hand and his little pipe with his right. He did this for his own reasons, of course, but plainly he was a fine racy young man of upper birth in the Provençal pecking order, with long bones and a disdainful shy look. My girls seemed dizzy when they met him on the six flights of stairs, and when he started to practice his little pipe and make muffled taps on his tambour, they turned paler.

I felt very sorry for them. They were listening to sounds that had been wandering through the air in Greece, more than two thousand years ago, and then had gone on relentlessly in the country we were living in, through all the dark ages until our lighter years.

The lonely boy piped and drummed, of course not knowing what he was doing to all of us on the other side of the wall, and then he went away. But the rhythm of his music is still in my heart, and probably my girls', although I have never asked them.

—*Glen Ellen, California, 1979*

22

One Verse of a Song

It is too soon to write the real story of the house I lived in for a long time in northern California. The Judith Clancy drawing shows more of its western Victorian dignity than I can, and its strength and beauty, and the honesty of birds in trees and tolerant cats dozing beneath.

When my two young girls and I bought the house, in about 1954, it lay under a passing cloud of sadness and decay. I went into the long dim kitchen once, and at the end of a big table sat a skeleton of an old woman, staring remotely at trays and platters and plates of rotting food that neighbors had brought to her for countless unheeded days. Books of philosophy and early feminist writings were tumbled on shelves and piled in corners on the floor. Over the sorrow and the stench, I felt the vitality of her and of her house, and I was by nature unafraid of ghosts.

Before long she was snoozing off in a kind cousin's warm clean sheets, and my girls and I were scraping and painting and airing her fine old house.

Below the high first floor there was a half-underground basement that ran the full length of the building, as was the custom in
Napa Valley when many of its settlers were Italians who wanted to
store their wines and olive oils and grains in dark cool places. The
floor was partly paved, with little runnels in it for the rainy seasons,
and the thick foundations, about forty inches high, were of local
stone, often dry-laid by the Chinese laborers, a dime a dozen in St.
Helena in 1870 (or more correctly, about sixty cents for a twelve-
hour day). The workmen laid clumsy cement tops on their stubby
walls, which later made fine shelves for our plates and books.

After the house was aired and brightened according to our
tastes, and a few ghosts made their peace with us, we invited some
Boy Scouts and 4-H buddies to dig out the half of the basement
that had been left walled but unpaved. Vague legends were used
as bait: the old doctor who had built the place, a miserly eccentric,
was said to have buried treasures under trees and in heaps of
rubble . . .

The young people worked like stevedores, bolstered by
healthy snacks and swigs and dreams of hidden gold, and they did
dig up some artifacts that pleased me, no matter how disappointing
they may have been to the diggers. There was a Chinese paring
knife, with a teakwood handle inlaid in pewter and a strong pure
blade of steel. It sharpens well, and I use it almost daily. There was
also a crude but lovely rice bowl. And there was a tall six-sided
bottle of brown glass, with a tiny neck. The budding medicos and
farmers who uncovered it assured us, with discreet titillation, that
it had probably once held a specimen fetus, coming as it did from
the old doctor's leavings, and I never asked them how much more
than a cobweb could have passed through that opening. I still have
the jar, a handsome thing on a high shelf.

In the basement we installed several windows, short and wide,
of what was then called cathedral glass, almost the color of the
bottle. The rest of the dirt floor was paved, always with the artfully

graded little runnels for possible flooding in the rainy seasons, because we were below the gravity-flow level. We put in a half-bath. Part of the space turned into a kind of wine-cellar pub, and there were beds for four people, like couches, in other stony places. We put thick hemp mats on the floors, and hung a few translucent bamboo screens between some of the beams that held up the whole house, and there were books everywhere on the wonderful wide ledges.

The big stone base for the fireplace upstairs stood in the pub, a handsome wall of stonework more probably laid by an Italian mason than by the Chinese. And there was the hulk of the old gas furnace, with five ugly asbestos arms taking heat to the first floor. It was infallible, never-failing, ready to take over at the slightest drop in temperature and quiescent as a happy dog in the hot dry months, so that the basement itself stayed warm or cool as needed —a magic trick!

Much of our time, during the years we lived in St. Helena, was spent down there. It was fine for good bashes and dinner parties and meetings. It was easy to bring edibles down from the kitchen, and the wine was already there! And soon after we moved into the house I found myself working more and more in the basement, so that finally everything I was pondering on was down there, close beside the bed I grew to prefer to all others in the lighter rooms upstairs.

The main floor had two bedrooms for my children. Now and then, as they gradually left for schools and as we all gravitated into the basement for various reasons connected with peace and its components, the girls gave their rooms to the people who some-times came to stay with us. Now and then I myself would sleep in one of them, for a change or if the runnels were gurgling after a storm. But up in the attic was my official bedroom, even after I sank permanently into the basement.

Like it, the attic ran the whole length and width of the house.

The roof sloped sharply to the eaves, of course, but there was plenty of fine stand-up room down the middle. The front part was partitioned with heavy chicken wire from the rest of the generous space, and people told us that this may have been to contain some relatives of the dotty old lady from whom we had bought the house. We knew better: her sons had once raised pigeons there, to fly in and out the tiny lamp window, and we had cleaned out a lot of feathery old dung, certainly not human.

At the other end of the attic, looking west, the handy sons had built a fine room over the back porch below, with a whole wall of windows and plenty of room for my big bed and many bookcases, and a few old trunks and cases set against the redwood walls. It was a good nest for my nightlife, until with the force of time and gravity I sank more and more into the dim quiet depths of the basement. I always went up there, though, to be alone when I needed to.

In between those two levels, on the first floor, the house was airy, filled with clear colors and the lacy flicker of light through bamboo leaves. The woodwork everywhere was flat white, and the floors were of large black and white tiles (vinyl, but more than adequate). The ceilings were all fifteen feet high. The walls in the front room were "museum gray," fine for pictures and long bookcases and old rugs, and there was an excellent, if rather ugly, brick fireplace at the far end as one entered from the little hallway. The front door, with a dark yellow glass panel in it, had a funny handbell built in, with a loud mean ring. It was really a *good* room.

The kitchen behind it was good too, and almost as big. The walls were dark green; the furniture was brown; everything else was white. It matched a copy of one of my favorite Braques above one of the two long bookcases, opposite the kitchen counter and across from the generous table, which often seated ten at a pinch, or preferably six or eight.

Off the two main rooms were the children's, with a bath and

a toilet where the plumbing was old-fashioned but adequate. And to the left of the front door was a small office (doubtless where the doctor had pulled teeth and set bones and so on), which after my short happy tenure there with my typewriter became the glory hole. Extra copies of books, wrapping supplies, Christmas decorations, picture frames too bulky to carry up the narrow stairs to the attic, boxes that might someday be useful—they all went into this family reservoir, which by some miracle kept its own chaotic tidiness.

Plainly, it is hard to know which room in the house was the best, the most pleasing, but perhaps it was the back porch, under my attic nest. It too had been build by the handy boys who'd kept pigeons, and the many windows and the seams in the flimsy walls jammed and leaked and bulged now and then, but we forgave everything for the bright welcome that seemed to spread out from it the minute anyone came up the narrow steep back stairs and inside, no matter for the first or the hundredth time. Its long row of windows looked out into a giant fig tree. The walls were a light clear yellow. The curtains were of a soft red plaid, and the linings of all the open supply shelves and china cupboards were of the same red. The floor was black and white, of course. There were two good old rocking chairs. We kept table linens in a big highboy. There were racks for fruits and vegetables. The place was reassuring.

People grew used to the fact that the outside house would look shaggy and shabby while we lived there, and they came to feel easy within it. Outside, it was a soft faded mustard color, half-hidden by carefully controlled masses of Peking bamboo. Inside, it was a charmed mixture of light and color, where the air was always sweet and the leaves made fine delicate curtains against the wavery old glass in the tall windows. The fire drew well on the hearth, in winter. In summer, the basement was a cool dim windless cavern.

Other people now take care of the Dear Old Lady, as a lot of us call her, and they have made her look tidier than we ever did, certainly. She will outlive us all. Of that I am sure. And as long as I can, I'll sing my own songs of love and thanksgiving for the lives she helped us lead.

—Glen Ellen, California, 1980

23
Bugs

The last two days have been odd, so when I turned down my bed I was not surprised to see a small black insect hide deftly in a fold of the sheet. I shook it out and it hid again, three times. Finally I brushed it roughly and listened to hear it hit the tile floor minutely, so that I knew it was not in the bed anymore.

Then I went into the bathroom, a warm dim elegant place, and on the edge of the washbowl there was something dark, like a postage stamp. I looked closely at it, and its large eyes looked back at me, asking for pity or at least some understanding. It was a small frog.

I stared down at him, perhaps six inches from his anxious little face. Sometimes a frog seems mostly face and hind legs, but this little one was like a puzzled child, proportionately. His throat pulsed silently, and my own heart went along with it.

I knew that neither of us wanted him to stay like a stain on the edge of the porcelain bowl, any more than we wanted him to smell of my skin when I touched his. I got a piece of thin paper tissue, the kind put in bathrooms nowadays, and picked him up softly. I kept my grasp light but firm, and looked down at him in the paper, with his little legs spread out helplessly, and his mouth half open. He was colored black on his back, and a pearly gray on his belly.

We seemed to go out to the big fern together. He did not move, but I knew from the vibrations in my hand that he was alive and optimistic. Once near the big sturdy plant in its box, he was ready to leave, and I dropped him almost nonchalantly into the tender new leaves at its heart. I heard him land.

This was a strange encounter, not the first in my bathroom but perhaps significant because the last two days had made me confront other visitors. Yesterday, for instance, I turned out a vigorous earwig and a sturdy spider from my bed, when I plumped the pillows in the morning. Then there were two earwigs copulating in the washbasin when I wanted to wash my face and hands.

"Go *on*," I said. "Get along. This is my house. Please get out."

Later on in the day I washed a lot of vegetables, and flushed the sink well, and everything was spotless, except that a couple of hours later I went back to the kitchen and a fairly large slug was wearily making its way up the porcelain side. I dislike slugs in a way that is perhaps atavistic, as well as possibly Freudian, but I found myself speaking to this poor bewildered thing as if he could know what I was saying. "I'm going to pick you up in a paper towel," I said, "and because you can't possibly survive in this climate and air, no matter where you came from, I'll put you into the trash can, and the men are coming tomorrow to empty it and you will be gone."

I did pick up this poor thing, trying not to feel how his long body tensed into a kind of rubber in my papered fingers.

This is the day for confronting the crawlers and nibblers, I said. What are they telling me? Perhaps tomorrow I'll know. But that day is now, today, and I am thinking of the desperate patience of that little frog or perhaps toad as he sat waiting for me to get him out of the bathroom. He did seem to know that I would come, much more clearly than I myself could guess. And when I arrived, meaning as I did to refresh myself, he told me clearly that I could help him get the hell out of walls-tiles-windows into a big potted fern and then his own eternity.

There was another hint, yesterday, about the need of insects and other creatures to communicate with human beings. I wear what are now called panty hose: filmy or stretched tights that pull up over the hips, making stockings on the legs of bipeds. I got into some as usual, in the morning, and went out of the bathroom. In a minute or two, though, I felt something nibble at my left hip. I hit it and perhaps scratched vaguely at it, thinking it was perhaps an arthritic twinge, and realized that there was something between the stocking and my skin. I ripped everything down, without ceremony since I was alone, and felt a wetness around what I pulled out: a tiny black limp creature, *not* a beetle or a tick.

I felt shocked, and did not examine the plainly dead critter, except to note that it was small, black, and had once had feelers or tentacles coming from one end of its body. Where had it come from? Why did it get into my panty hose? And how? Where had it been until it got there?

All this made me shake out my pillows last night, in an almost smiling way. I wondered mildly about spring, and moisture, and so on. I thought of a book or story read long ago, about ants and how organized they were. I thought more definitely about the volcanic ash that was sifting and falling and drifting from Mount St. Helens, and about the Pacific mountains that were shaking. I wondered and I still do about what signals we are getting that there may be a change in priorities.

At this point I can get rid of a slug in my kitchen sink, an earwig under my pillow, a small sad-eyed froglet in my bathroom washbowl—but I think they are telling us something that is very hard to hear. Is it a question of plumbing, or one of a more universal nature?

—Glen Ellen, California, 1980

24

Light Sleeper

Today is Sunday, and for a pleasant change in my schedule, there will be nobody here. At least no one is marked in the book. I could lie abed if I wanted to and for a long time I did. I think it was about ten o'clock when I got up. It did not matter, because the night had been long and easy and sweet: a few good dreams, and an unusually intense enjoyment about it, so that I lay mostly in a half-sleep or quietly awake, in order to enjoy it. And I wanted it to last, to keep my gentled sensations sliding me along toward what would be left of the horizontal day. Once on my feet again, I well knew, such passive sensuous pleasure would perforce change, no matter how positively.

The main thought, if such rambling snoozy contemplation can be called thinking, was that I am lucky to be a light sleeper, and not someone who through habit and other tricks of nature believes that anything but eight hours of complete unconsciousness means insomnia. One turn or toss, three minutes of alertness after a dog's bark, or the inward tweak of an outraged bowel muscle, and such a miserable creature honestly feels that wakefulness, the bane of honest healthy believers in Law and Order, has invaded him. Sleeplessness is an enemy. Anything except full dormancy is frightening. It means illness, or even guilt. A pill, a pill! Doctor, help me. I can't sleep—I turn and toss. I sweat.

All this is nonsense to me. I welcome dreams. I've never bowed to the word *insomnia,* and I often lie awake for many hours with real pleasure, knowing that some day or some night I will sleep again. I feel fortunate . . .

—*Glen Ellen, California, 1980*

25

The Hot Look
of July

After the sun went down it grew cool and sweet, and across the little valley I watched, as I do almost every night, the darkening high ridge of desolate craggy mountains between me and the ocean, and then the nearer somewhat greener hills of a county park with easy trails for junior citizens and those in the "golden years," as our local brochures say to anyone who looks at them.

It felt fine to be in this world again, and not waiting for it to come around, as it seems essential to do for those two or three hours of near nirvana in the late afternoons. We lie naked and spread-eagled on our sheets, inertly waiting to come back.

Across the valley, an ugly bright hard light comes on after the sun sets, and I did not realize until tonight that it is set to ward off prowlers who might rightly surmise that the hillside property is largely vacant, owned by rich occasional tenants. I always try to block out this light as I watch indolently, peacefully, from my balcony chair. I look instead at a familiar, the big owl who sits for a long time on my one tall pole in the meadow and then suddenly is not the top part of the pole but a great silent dreadful swoop of wings and the end of a little mole or mouse in the sloping meadow below. It is a time for carelessness, and I may hear a small cry as the hawk at the top of a dead tree down in the meadow swoops for another creature and lifts him up in his lethal claws. But there is a general air of watchful surcease.

Tonight, though, there was too much activity along the highway that runs down on the other side of the meadows, under the first low range of hills that make the park. The park has two entrances, one into the grounds and one into a higher-up place that is occasionally lit at night with one big yard globe, as if somebody might come in later. The globe is further up and to the right of the ugly light.

Tonight, as the sky faded from a fine clear hot sunset into cool darkness, I saw that the ugly bright light had been set so that it went off at perhaps five-minute intervals, and that when it came on, after that lovely nonlight, it was at first a small bluish glow that turned within perhaps two minutes into the lean cruel white light I had come to avoid. It would go off, then glow into brightness again.

As I watched, a car came down the park road and slowly turned right, to the south as often happens, but this time I noticed that before it eased into the patchy weekend traffic, it blinked its lights twice.

Then a car that passed it coming south blinked its "far" lights, and after the first car got out onto the highway, the second car turned around and headed north.

At the mouth of the other driveway down from the ridge of low hills, a car that had come down without any lights, from the house that sometimes burned the ugly bright light all night, suddenly put on its high beam, so that its lights streamed across the highway and up into our meadow just as the car that had turned around passed it. That car blinked twice and went on. The car from up the hill kept its lights on as if it were waiting to come out carefully onto the highway. Finally it turned off its lights completely.

By now dark had almost come. I sat on the balcony feeling a little like the owl on the telephone pole, the hawk on the branch, waiting.

After perhaps two minutes, the darkened car flashed on its lights as if it had just come down the highway, and turned south and went on out of sight, but as it passed, the old light up on the hill that had been going off and on at planned intervals for at least an hour suddenly flashed out strongly three times: Eeee-Eeee-Eeee. The car blinked its headlights once, and disappeared.

I waited, but everything looked as it always did from my balcony on a hot July night. The new moon was almost down, and a jet plane lowered itself gently toward the city, coming perhaps from very far away. A few cars went up and down the old highway. I thought that maybe tomorrow I would hear on the early radio news that a big drug bust had been pulled off, or that child abuse rings were rampant again, or that maybe in twenty more minutes we would not have much more time because some current Strangelove was loose, pushing buttons.

A supper of cold salmon and blueberries with cream tasted fine, if you care about those things, and I'll sleep well, except that I wonder if heat has anything to do with people giving each other signals with their yard lights and car lights. I doubt that there will be any news tomorrow about this.

—Glen Ellen, California, 1980

26

Interviews—II

It is difficult not to feel compulsive about this strange experience. I have been thinking about it for some twenty-two hours, trying to arrange and observe it.

A few days ago a young journalist came to interview me for her magazine, and then called me (I thought this was unusually courteous in the profession as it now exists) to ask if her photographer might telephone.

I agreed, of course. A day later Sandra L. called, and I invited her to come at 12:00 yesterday. She sounded young and pleased to break bread with me. It was agreed that she would come at noon.

The morning of our meeting, she called to ask if it would be all right for her to come at 11:30, since she had another engagement. It was not too convenient for me but I was agreeable, and hustled a bit to get the table set and the soup ready.

She did not come until 12:20, with no apology.

She was a very tall thin girl, in jeans of course, and wearing the kind of crimped-out dark blond hair that was stylish last year after *Annie* became a stage success: parted in the middle so that it went straight sideways and out, a real frizzzzzz. Her pretty face, which was almost masked, was like a child's, with resentful eyes and a bobbed nose and a mouth just beginning to learn.

Sandra unloaded a lot of tripods and other stuff.

She was an arrogant rude girl; I'm sure she has never been shown how to be anything else. She was very defensive, on the watch for "grown-up" slurs and put-downs. She affected a tiny mocking smile, which I caught now and then in the wild brush of frizzzzzz. I thought, Here is one of my godchildren. She had the tall lean insolence, the ashy light hair, the pale hating eyes.

She strolled in, moving like a beautiful giraffe with a very small head. I showed her the "two-room palazzo." This was to let her know that the house was hers to use for her camera, but she seemed to have no reaction. She asked me to change into something other than what I was wearing, which was neat and tidy and exactly what I wear all the time (except in bed).

I was so taken aback, to put it archaically, that I asked her what she wanted me to wear. The thought of changing into "costumes" shocked me so much that I decided to go along with it. She followed me into my clothes closet, and chose a djellaba that I've had for many years and seldom worn.

To my own amazement I stripped and got into a long black silk slip and the swimmy cotton thing, and put on flat silk shoes. After that I posed—*posed.*

The girl shot me in blinding light, on the west balcony, in ridiculous poses (or so they seemed to me).

She talked in a rather muttering insolent way as she fussed with her elegant equipment, and I learned that she was a Stanford grad and had majored in psychology and had a boyfriend.

But mostly she kept saying in a very quiet rude way that she had never worked with a subject who was so plainly hostile and quarrelsome. Such comments were mixed in with more casual talk. But I felt that she was deft at this game, and well practiced in taunting and trying to hurt the people she knew. There was also quite a lot of racial or ethnic resentment—her *name*, which she had first told me almost giggling with ethnic apology. And in a monotone along with her chatter, she asked if I really hated her. "I have never before worked with such a terrible subject," she said again.

I already knew that I should never have obeyed her demand to shoot me in another outfit, and I was cross with my weakness. She said, in the midst of her monologue, "I don't know why you are so antagonistic, so hateful."

I said once, "I am not. Let's get on with the job."

She went off into a speech about spoiled people, mostly female, who want only to look beautiful or intelligent. Finally I asked her what course she had taken in psychology. This really aggravated her, and she snapped at me. I felt somewhat alarmed, and excused myself and changed into a warmer djellaba. She took some more shots. Her small face behind all the kinked hair was sullen, and she made no response to my mild questions: Are you freelancing? Do you like the work? Would you like to live up here? Or down south? It was like being with a child who wants to punish you but does not know how. I imagined her keeping up this quiet sulky monotone while helpless parents and even doctors wrung their hands.

Once my cat Charlie came in, to sniff her, and she said, "I suppose you want some shots with him in your arms?" She implied that this was not only what all subjects like, but a last resort. I said, almost as casually but with no sneer, "No. I'm leading a crusade to forbid all aging writers from being photographed clutching their cats. We all are. Colette started it, perhaps, and it should end with her."

She asked blankly, staring out from her wall of hair, "Who's Colette?"

I was surprised by her interest, and almost caught her small blue eye, but lost it when I said that Colette was a writer at the turn of the century. She shrugged: what century and who cared?

She was very abrupt and bossy in her work, which she accomplished with a great deal of fuss about the tripods and light meters. "Turn this way. No. This won't be any good." She kept walking impatiently toward me with a meter and pressing it into my shoulder to see it tick. I felt like a piece of repugnant meat.

Later she drank two glasses of fruit juice, and when we finally sat down to what I thought was a good little lunch of Chinese-style vegetable soup, she drank about three spoonsful and ate half a slice of brown bread and refused the bowl of seeded black and white grapes that followed. She ate half a cookie. She was being true to some inner compulsion about her job, I said to myself.

A couple of times she peered out at me and said coolly, in a quiet trained voice, "I've never had such a venomous cruel assignment."

I said, "I honestly don't know what has gone wrong here." I hemmed and hawed a bit, because I could not tell her flat out that she was a rude spoiled brat. I refused to let her reduce me to a frustrated dither, which I felt that she must love doing to her parents and her friends.

After she left, she came back into the house, pushing past me. "I always leave something—I'll check again," she said, and went into the two rooms and onto the balconies, to see if she had left any of her luxurious equipment behind. It was a pathetic gesture. She did not like me because I represented a job, an obligation, a responsibility. I did not like her because she was arrogantly rude. And she was not yet mature, if ever she will permit herself to be. She could not be warm and trusting and overt because hostility had for a long time been her weapon against the world. (And "the world," to her, probably means parents and older people like me: *enemies.*)

I felt sorry about all this, after she had gotten all her gear into her sleek little car and had wheeled angrily away. I had never experienced such open disdain and anger in a professional meeting, and I wondered if I was growing crotchety. This is said to happen in one's later years, and certainly I feel remotely impatient of younger people's prejudices. But I had never met such an insolent young person. I wondered about her as I cleared the uneaten food from the table. (At least she was wise enough not to ingest food while angry! And she was indeed slim and quite lovely, except for her aura of disdain.)

I asked myself where I'd gone wrong, how I'd punched the bad button. I felt, early on, that she had made all her abrasive remarks before. But they were new in my experience with professional photographers. Did she resent my nonchalance and nonposing for her camera?

I'll probably never know, because I forget the magazine she was freelancing for, and doubt that a copy will be sent to me. I know that I am not photogenic now, as the pull of gravity forces my face downward. But I also know that I like to encourage younger people to take pictures, write reports, make themselves wanted if they are ambitious. Most of the ones who come here for pictures and so-called interviews are in their twenties and early thirties, and they enjoy the experience.

But this girl! I must ask a "head doctor" about her quiet monologue of ridicule and disdain. She was infinitely scornful and supercilious of everything in my house, and especially of me, and soon I understood that her quiet hatred was intended to make me afraid of her.

But why? Why use me as an object of scorn, in her insecurity?

As I now see it, she was trying to punish me, for being old and better known and perhaps more balanced than she. Through me, she was punishing her parents, her doctors, her employers. Most of all, probably, she was whipping herself, punishing her own ego, suffering.

At this point in my attempt to talk about this odd prickly meeting I feel very bored. Why do I bother to explain it? Perhaps it is because I have always assumed that when I permit a journalist or photographer to come here, and invite him or her or them to break bread with me, I am being welcoming and warm, and hope they will feel relieved and easier. But this poor soul was apparently so filled with distaste or scorn that she could not even swallow my good soup!

Ah, well, she may have forgotten the whole assignment by now. I have not, but I am no longer obsessed with it. I remember her tall lithe young body, her small pinched sneering face behind the mop of dyed tortured hair. I hear, but very faintly, her questions interspersed with the monologue on her camera work: Why are you so hostile to me? Are you scared of my camera? Do you mind if I show all your wrinkles? Do you hate being an unknown writer? Why do you feel such hatred for me?

Little could she know.

—Glen Ellen, California, 1980

27
Unsuspected

On a trip to San Francisco in 1933, Rex and I stopped to visit Mrs. Fisher, my mother-in-law. She was like Edith, but she had continued to play the piano. Edith had not. As we were leaving, we turned back for a forgotten something—camera or briefcase or or or—and found that Mrs. Fisher had already gone into her tiny room filled with a grand piano and was playing a torrent of exquisite lush syllables of sound: Bach.

Rex was literally transfixed. We stood like statues out on the walk. I looked at him with a new and wonderful astonishment. For in that moment, he was not my father, but a man who loved his wife—my mother—and who felt lost because she no longer played the Schumann, Chopin, Brahms he had worshipped as a callow young editor.

And now another woman, much less fortunate in some ways —a minister's wife and not an editor's, but with much the same cultural upbringing—was playing beautiful music to soothe her own soul, alone in her small room with a weak boring old man as her husband, and the children behind her.

My father had his wife, my mother. She had four children too, but she no longer cared enough to touch the piano keys.

We stood outside the little house where my first father-in-law panted and prayed through his last pastoral assignment, and I found it hard to look at my father as he stood immobile on the path, listening to the wonderful waterfall of sound that fell on us.

Then we went to knock again at the door, and the tall full-bodied woman spoke courteously to us and found what we had left behind.

We left like awkward schoolchildren. A few times, many years later, my father asked me if I remembered the time we went back and she was playing. His face was full of light. I wished for both of us that Mother had not stopped.

—*Glen Ellen, California, 1981*

 28

Visitation

Last night when the sun went down I sat for a long time on the west balcony. It was the end of the fifteenth day of heat over a hundred degrees in this valley, and I felt tired and hollow-headed. My cat Charlie lay on the cool tiles, after a late supper.

We both heard what sounded like a kitten, mewing weakly from down near Herger's Pit. Charlie was immediately alert, with his ears far forward. I stood up. We listened to two more periods of little cries, and when he became restless and worried I let him out into the courtyard. He sat on the wall, lashing his tail at first and then settling into a wary crouch.

There was no more crying, and I leaned back in my chair, to watch the slow flight of the present satellite toward what I think of as Jenner—north-northwest and right into the last sunset color.

There was no sound from Charlie, but suddenly there was a scrabbling and I saw a black cat hanging on the thin edge of the balcony, trying to get in through the thick Plexiglas shield. His eyes glared at me for a second, and then he fell back to the ground, which is at least ten feet below.

I went fast to check on what had happened. Charlie, when he was young, had dropped off the balcony a couple of times, but had never come up the bare straight wall to jump in.

On the ground, in dimming light, I saw a young cat, black as black. He looked up at me with eyes that seemed to fix mine into a clear focus, and yelled firmly. Charlie started a low warning sound from the courtyard wall.

I felt helpless: my cat would never permit this one to come into his domain, as I knew from past painful experience, so it would be wise to let them discuss it without interference. I went back to my chair, and a view of the sharpening horizon as the hills turned black.

Then the new cat leaped up onto the outer ledge of the balcony again, and hung there, crying frantically, before he dropped down onto the ground. I tried to shift the Plexiglas so that he could not possibly come through the space between it and the wall at the end, but I could not close the two-inch gap, and I went fast to telephone two neighbors to ask if they knew about a half-grown tar-black cat. Mr. King did not answer. Mr. Burns knew nothing about such an animal, and I told him I was sorry to have bothered him, for it was then about 9:30.

When I went back to the balcony, the cat had not only gotten through the gap but was in the kitchen, eating the crumbs of Charlie's supper. I said several loud *Nos,* and he scuttled out, and I made a new bowl of fresh food from the icebox as fast as I could, and we seemed to meet as if by arrangement on the balcony, where he ate furiously, growling without anger.

I closed the door into the house from the balcony, and very soon Charlie was crouched behind it—poor dumb fellow, so slow to figure out that if the interloper was not on the ground that he had been watching from the courtyard wall, then he must be inside!

The new cat was truly beautiful, pure black, probably a mixture of Siamese and Burmese, perhaps six months old, with good manners even though so plainly desperate for food. I sat silently in my chair, trying not to encourage his staying but wanting very much to. Charlie is a complete tyrant. It was impossible for the stranger to stay, but this fine creature had already insisted on coming and eating, and I believe firmly that when a cat chooses to do something, it will happen. I have proved this foolish theory more than once, and I tingled with wonder that it might happen again and that this time Charlie, who is now in his twelfth or thirteenth year, would accept a bold beautiful newcomer.

The black intruder finished his dinner slowly. Charlie fumed in the living room, crouched behind the glass door. Then the younger cat hissed directly at my friend; it was the loudest hiss I have ever heard, much like the sound of a rattlesnake. Charlie stopped growling and fuming and pretending to protect his territory, and I thought for a second that perhaps he would bow down to time and aging and and and . . .

The intruder hissed again, long and firm. There was silence. Then he leaped like a nonchalant flash of black lightning over the balcony railing. I saw his fine young body fly through the sky, and heard it land lightly far below.

I left his bowl until this morning, and then washed it so that my cat would not sniff another's presence in it when next I used it for him. I closed the door onto the balcony, so that Charlie would not fret about the other cat's having made it his own for a few minutes.

Today all seems tranquil, and the end of the unprecedented heat wave, historically both too early and too long, seems here, at least for two or three days. I feel less light-headed and much relieved. But the night visit was so strange, after such a long time of heat, that I thought I'd better get it onto paper before it went into legend and not a straight report.

I am eager for tonight's sunset on the balcony. Meanwhile Charlie is his usual demanding but unruffled self, and probably has the whole situation in hand. I think I want the young black stranger to come back. But he is plainly a con artist, taking what he gets (even by force) and then moving out. And now I wonder if, after the long heat, I was quite in focus about watching a half-grown cat leap up at least ten feet, three times, and cling to the balcony edge and finally come in and eat, and then cow Charlie.

Charlie was pretending to be asleep when I went out to the balcony. He jumped at once onto my knees, and I knew that he had made it clear that the stranger should move on.

I felt sorry—such a beautiful seeker for a place to stay awhile. But my cat told him that he was an arrogant and even detestable upstart, no matter how soft I might be about not turning him away. So I sighed and accepted, too lazy perhaps to urge the wanderer into what would probably be a miserable situation. He was wise to move on, and I feel certain that if he dodges road traffic he will find a more welcoming place. I feel equally sure that if the conditions are not to his taste, he will move on—not fat, but never too lean.

—*Glen Ellen, California, 1981*

29

Recovery

The process of growing well after being unwell is an odd
one and has always interested me. For instance, tonight is the
twenty-second day after I was given a complete new hip on my
right side, at my request.

All has gone almost phenomenally well, probably because I
had faint and few qualms about the minor side effects of hospital-
ization, and chose after some deliberation to try for even partial
mobility rather than a few more years of painful frustrated "cop-
ing" from bed or chair. The thought of being attended to, and
dependent upon, other more active people was literally untenable.
Yes, everything went with unusual smoothness. For instance, the
actual surgery took about two and a half hours rather than the
expected five. Only three one-pint transfusions were needed instead of the five or six that had been readied. And so on.

I feel strong and firm, and except for small times of annoyance
when I drop things, or occasional twinges of peculiarly horrible

pain when I am careless about doing something that I know I must not do, I am cheerful and courteous, and I keep myself well combed and washed.

But tonight I would like to be changed into another being. It is almost dark, and the air is cooling after unusual heat, and very still. I sit in the big ugly Victorian armchair that has been brought in from the living room, with a hard pillow to keep me from bending the hip at a right angle, so that I am leaning back awkwardly. I am not too hot. I am not unclean—that is, I don't want to make the effort to shower and dry and so on. I feel all right in my skin.

But I wish I could be transported somehow to my bed at the other end of the room. Perhaps a perfume would make me lean back on the cruel old cushion, and I would smile a sweet docile stupid smile, one that would say, Yes . . . Now. And then I would be lying naked, flat, on the bed. At least three very old witches, almost as gray and thin as smoke, would pull off my canvas shoes and hold up my two bony long thin feet and say, "Ah, yes, ah, yes," and they would blow softly on them, so that they would smell as if they were made of exquisite wax and not hot cotton and foot sweat.

So as I lie cool and naked on the sheet, my feet, fresh and sweet, seem to finish me off down there, thousands of fathoms or miles down there. Then the two other smoke people—witches, fairies, angels—smooth my skin, and through my skin my nerves and muscles and then the bones and then the marrow and gristle and whatever else it is that holds us into one position or another, and there is not a sound, except outside the summer song of the wee toads in the few hidden mud packs under the rocks. There is an invisible singing.

The smoke-thin smoke-clear fingers smooth me, and I lie on the cool sheet smiling a little, like an animal or perhaps like smoke.

There are three of them, very see-through, like the angel Timmy painted who wept to see one green seed sprout from burnt-egg earth. It was Birth she wept at. I do not want to be born again, and the three smoke women do not wish it for me either, but there is nothing to do about it and they keep on silently rubbing my long tired body. By now it is thin, but I do not feel at all sorry, except for the deformed arthritic knobs on my inner knees, which I have always (seven years?) found an insult.

They came unexpectedly in Marseille, when Norah and I went up and down the old iron stairway at least once a day, on our way past the Vieux Port. (I forget now how many steps there were— perhaps 170. They clanged. During a bad mistral they swayed.) And one day I walked toward the mirror in my room and saw that on either side of my inner knees there was a soft meaningless bulge. I was astonished. I had always had straight legs. Later, in St. Helena again, I was told they were the natural result of my protective system giving my aging knees a bit of padding for taking that iron stair so often. I still have them, but since nobody sees my form now, I do not resent them. Tonight, as the three old smoke witches smooth me, one laughs or perhaps only smiles that it is all right. My good body has been kind to me, she says. I know.

And they keep on rubbing, in an almost intangible but completely knowing way, the way I sometimes press exactly the right nerves in the back of my cat when he has eaten a fresh kill and comes slowly to sit by my chair.

I hate him at first, and hold my breath, not wanting to breathe the fresh gut smells of the dead mole or gopher. Finally I lean a little, so that my arm touches the small of his back as he sits on the floor. Omnivore, carnivore, I curse him softly, and then I touch exactly the right nerves and muscles down toward the end of his spine, and know that I have communicated with him in a way neither of us had planned.

In the same way the smoky old old—well, are they witches? ghosts? nurses?—in the same way I am not here but I am on my cool bed, and they—they have touched or brushed or breathed upon or in some way made the tendons and even the flesh of my tattered body feel right again.

This is what recovery means, I suppose. I know that soon I'll be strong and firm. Tonight I like to know that even while the lights are still on and I talk and eat and awkwardly ready myself for a night that is not yet a good night, a rest that is not yet rest, there are the smoke ladies. I have not yet had to call upon them, and I hope I never do. But tonight might be a good time to try.

—Glen Ellen, California, 1981

30
Rewriting

Here is something about semantics and ethics, and it interests me enough to try to describe it.

I was trying to reread a story I wrote about thirty years ago for my two little girls, who were the protagonists along with a fine four-legged friend called Boss Dog. Several times I used the word *gay* to describe him, because that is exactly what he was, in my vocabulary and my children's and I assume his. He was merry, funny, giddy, happy, and in every sense of the word gay. And my father had been like that, and the children's father. They were very gay happy people.

But now I was having to change that word every time it came up in the story about Boss Dog and my children. I was by all current laws both written and spoken and even unspoken being forced to accept the fact that a gay person is now strictly a homosexual male living or professing a "lifestyle" frowned upon by born-again Christians and condoned with brotherly compassion by the self-styled broader-minded people of the western part of Earth.

So I was chugging along at this ridiculous bow to publishing ethics and so on, when the telephone rang and a loud passionate weeping flooded me, and I was no longer a white Anglo-Saxon something-or-other but a horrified female facing untrammeled Jewish grief.

Oh-oh-oh! A-hoo, a-hoo (e-heu, e-hue??). He's dead. Dead in my arms last night. Oh, a-hoo, a-hoo . . .

For many years I have lived with Orthodox and deeply religious Jews, although I am not one, and I heard what she said and I began to cry, not as openly as she did because I cannot, but in helpless (Anglo-Saxon?) silence. Then I asked questions and learned that my dear friend Rosie had indeed gasped, leaned onto her breast, smiled, and died.

Oh, Rosie, she cried out. A-hoo, a-hoo . . .

She was getting a little out of hand, my trained self told me while I tried to stop shaking and throbbing at the shock of Rosie's not *being* here in this part of the world anymore.

Oh, dear Anna, I said over her almost voluptuous and enjoyable wailing, he was such a wonderful gay person.

There was a complete hollow silence.

Then she said in a loud hard voice, *WHAT????*

I said that I meant that Rosie had been so happy, so merry, so . . .

Oh, she said, and then she went again into the a-hoo a-hoo, and I felt that everything was all right and I left her to her clustered relatives.

Of course I meant to finish the editing of the story about Boss Dog, but I have not felt like it. I keep wondering instead about fads in words and meanings. I would like to say that my father, or Rosie, or even Boss Dog, was a really gay fellow. But I cannot, because I have several close longtime friends who are "gay," not "gays," and I do not want ever to offend them. It did not enter my silly head that I could or would, until Rosie's widow suddenly stopped her genuine mourning wail: a-hoo, a-hoo . . .

—*Glen Ellen, California, 1982*

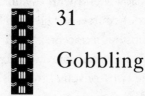

31

Gobbling

It is probably silly to form certain ideas or theories or even superstitions about anything at all, but since I seem to have reached a plateau of fairly tranquil recollection, for want of anything better to do, I'll note a few here.

One that occurred to me today, for a reason surely, but not one that seems worth tracing, is that I believe a great deal can be guessed about a person's ways of making love by his or her table manners—that is, by his way of eating.

My chances to observe this have not often been close or intimate, but I am fortunate that they have been good ones. And of course I observe much more than most people realize, so that often I feel quite willing to bet heavily after watching someone I'll almost certainly never meet or even see again, from across a restaurant for instance.

The connection between his table self and his bed self is largely one of speed. If he (and I use *he* because I am writing as a female)—if he eats slowly and with shy amazed looks at his companion, of either sex of course, he will be in bed as he was at table: shy, in a dream, almost an innocent.

If he eats slowly but with enjoyment, trying to share his pleasure in whatever the two consume, from fish and chips to beluga malossol caviar, and from ale in a stein to champagne, he will make love with the same sureness and delight and make sure that it is reciprocal.

On the other hand, and here I begin to prowl around the main action I have watched and been influenced by, if the lover gobbles, he will make love the same way, no matter what he is eating. He may not be gross or gluttonous, really, but later he will pounce upon his partner exactly as he has pounced upon his food. He will gobble like a hungry and usually happy dog, whether he is a registered thoroughbred or a mutt.

I am sure that one reason Charles Laughton was unforgettable when he played Henry VIII eating a roasted chicken is because Charles Laughton was that same man, and he knew it. He ate like a king who was a sated scavenger, who did not care if fat ran down his cheeks and glistened on his thick sensitive lips, who needed rich dainty flesh and coarse thick flesh and princesses and street sellers. Laughton was a real actor, which is why his king is still real. His personal pleasures were not those of King Henry, but I feel sure that in bed he could be as voracious and delicately vulgar as Henry was.

I am very glad that I never had to sleep with either of the two-in-ones. I did know a man for a long time whom I would have liked to be closer to than we ever were, but I found early in some forty years of good faithful friendship that he made love exactly as he ate, with excellent taste and style but so fast that it was almost as if it had not happened.

I cooked often for him, and it was much more fun than making love could have been, but I never knew how he could finish a dish or even a whole meal with such neat sensitive appreciative dispatch. Zipzipzip and the plates were clean, and not a crumb or spot anywhere! His manners were always excellent. His understanding was genuine, whether he tasted a fine sauce or a rare bottle of vintage wine.

But that was not right for making love and sleeping together, so I had to turn my back on such wishes because I wanted everything to last longer: I was not a truffle or a Romanée-Conti, but a nice slow voluptuous female. It was too bad, but what else was there to do but shrug fatalistically and vent my fleeting frustrations on the long slow preparation of a truffled hen, which I knew would disappear like magic in perhaps one-tenth of the time it had taken to roast it?

Of course plain gobbling is another matter, and one that does not interest me. I have never been attracted, sexually or otherwise, to people who eat grossly and without thought. In fact, most of the adult animals I have liked have eaten with what I like to think is appreciation and taste, no matter how noisily. Puppies, kittens, and two-legged people under eighteen or so are not yet appreciative of much more than the good feeling of a full stomach, but any young animal knows honest food from swill, and will not insult his budding taste if he is given any choice in the matter.

And I believe firmly that the way he eats will be the way he lives, whether it is as an unthinking hungry glutton or a fastidious libertine—or even a nice kindly small-town deacon. I have never known a man who fit into any of these three categories, but let me see him across the room and I'll know what he has been or is or will be in bed. His social class does not matter, any more than where he eats what he eats. I've shared meals with truck drivers and a couple of dukes, and although I have not slept with any of them, I honestly think that I know what it would have been like, because of the way they chewed and swallowed, and talked over and around and through what they put in their mouths.

Of course I cannot do anything to test this theory, given the realities of both time and space. In fact, as I expose it to possible view, I find it unworthy of speculation. I simply know it to be true! Perhaps somebody will think about it, and look across a room (crowded, of course) and see a stranger who picks up his fork and knife at exactly the right speed, and chews and swallows and then lets digestion take over at precisely the hoped-for rhythm. Then, as Brillat-Savarin would say, miracles may happen.

—Glen Ellen, California, 1983

32

Kicking Old Habits

I remember that I felt, when the doctors ordered that my father Rex should *absolutely* cease all use of salt in his diet, that I must evolve some substitutes. For why should a man at the end of his life live deprived and in fear? So I did my best with the food we ate, but since he was convinced that none of it would have any taste without salt, it took some time to return him to a fairly agreeable form of nourishment.

In the same way, both for him and for Dillwyn Parrish, I felt it sadistic to tell them to stop smoking. D. P. was so instructed about a year before his death, which had also been prognosticated. So why not let him continue? He did his best, with denicotinized cigarettes, but I think he would have been more self-assured, as he faced the inevitable death, if he had been able to lean on the crutch that had supported him for much of his life.

In the same way, Rex had lungs that were loaded with silt, and at the end of his life he breathed like a moth through blue lips, faintly, and sipped fastidiously at superlong cigarettes that had been studiously purified for him, and he continued to cough and to feel depleted.

This depletion of energy and interest was partly the fault of his age . . . maybe. But his lungs were clogged and perhaps fibroid, and why at seventy-six (or whatever he was) should a new regime be enforced? Why not let him go on coughing and wheezing?

My mother went through this too, but as a body confined mostly to bed for the last six years of her life, she had more energy and time to devote to the restrictions of her doctors.

They ordered NO SALT and prescribed for her a substitute that has since been proven dangerous and at times lethal. They said NO SMOKING, so after several decades of that nervous substitution for scratching or or or, she had nothing to do as she lay in bed, waiting for the next time she could take a drag at the oxygen machine or snap an ampoule of nitro.

And when, a few years ago, a friend stayed with me while her son and daughter-in-law and two adolescent grandchildren came from France, there were rare moments of complete accord when my friend smoked, voluptuously, one or two cigarettes, and sipped a weak brandy and water without ice. For the first time in perhaps forty years she was at ease, hidden, safe. (This is a supposition, of course.)

She came back last week, with her son. I noticed that he said triumphantly, when I remarked that she was not smoking, "CERTAINLY NOT! Cigarette smoke sickens me! She has absolutely forgone all that!" And she did not even sip a glass of wine at dinner, but in hopeless docility imitated her son when he loudly poured *water* into his glass. She stayed here with me, as before, but had bowed patiently to the dictates of the son. And now, without the relaxation of a cigarette, the pleasure of a little glass of wine, she goes back to France after her recent and unexpected widowhood, to live in a cottage near the son.

I don't advocate pandering drugs or alcohol to the aged, but I do think it is brutal to stop such calmatives toward the end of one's life, for reasons of health which should have been started fifty or seventy or eighty years earlier.

—Glen Ellen, California, 1983

33

Night Thoughts

A night thought does not happen often. When it does, it is of almost solemn importance, and should be heeded.

The trouble, though, is that its first clarity and simplicity become clouded and complicated almost as soon as it has happened, so that by the time it is set down, as I shall now try to do with my latest one, it is almost unrecognizable. Probably I should have got up into the cold November blackness before five—before dawn by several hours anyway—to write it straight from my subconscious or unconscious mind from whence it leaped into my sound sleep.

All night thoughts, in my own experience anyway, come as sharply and clearly as the sound of a silver bell or gong. They send me without warning into full consciousness, with no normal symptoms of interrupted sleep and blurred thoughts and blinking eyes. I am *awake*, perhaps with slightly hurried breathing or perhaps a fast pulse, but no sense of alarm or surprise. It is almost as if I had been shot through space, from one world to another, and words are simple and few in my mind, saying what I am waiting to hear.

Sometimes I can accept them as a solution to something that may or may not have been puzzling me but that I have had in my conscious mind. This was true, the last time, as I recalled a few hours after I first awoke. Earlier that night I had written to John Updike to thank him for a review he wrote in the *New Yorker* about my last book. I had put off writing to him, because I admire him very much, but I'd found when I finally read his review that he had looked at the book as if it were a personal or even autobiographical memoir, instead of the collection of old pieces about places that I'd meant it to be. Plainly this letter was working along in different levels of myself, hours after I had written it and signed it and recognized a sense of relief . . . a duty done. But before I dug up all this reasoning, the night thought was completely simple.

I was astonished. Everything I had been puzzled about in my reactions to the apparent "success" of the book was explained to me. By now I can't remember the thought exactly. I think it spoke to me as if I were a rather slow-witted and perhaps disobedient child. It said something like "You are disgusted and angry because you did not write what you should, for yourself, but you did what you were asked to do. Then you let it be changed into something else, and you did not protest. Then when critics praised it, you disdained their judgment, and when readers wrote to you, you felt disgusted by their acceptance of something you felt was a hoax, and you began to feel that they were stupid sheep to believe what they were told. You knew all along that the book was phony, not autobiography at all, not important. You are not a National Monument. You are not a stylist. You are not anything the readers want to believe you are. You are a docile fool."

Well, this is confused and wordy, not at all the clear firm

meaning that came ringing and singing so purely in the night thought. But its truth, even changed as it so quickly was, is there, and now I know why I cannot and do not and never will believe that *As They Were* is a good book.

I feel uncomfortable and impatiently amused that it is the first book that has ever had much other than critical attention paid to it. For the first time, I'll probably make some money beyond the initial advance. Reviews and fan mail continue to pour in, and it has been a best-seller now and then and here and there, and even good friends who should know me by now continue to disappoint me with their congratulations on my finding myself, at long last, in the limelight.

For years I have been sad and in a way embarrassed for my fellow writers who have had to write "idea books" for their editors and magazines. It has hurt me, as their peer, to know that when an editor has said, "Jane, or Bill, we need an article or a book on onions, or abortions, or or or . . . ," they have clicked their heels and in order to keep their jobs, or eat, or "get ahead," they have written an idea book or an idea piece. Ho hum.

But I have believed that I did not do that, did not have to do that, never would do that. And so when Judith suggested that I "put together" a book of short pieces about places, so that Knopf could print it and then, if it was any good at all, combine it with the two books on Aix and Marseille to make a three-book paperback about places in general, I agreed. I wanted the Aix and Marseille books to be reprinted, because a lot of people have asked how to get copies, and both are out of print.

I forgot how hard it is for me to look at old material, and almost at once I felt I could not possibly pull together any old stuff. But I was rather unwell, in a physical and mental slump, and I told myself that it would be good for me to prove that I could still function, somehow, if I did this job. But I was having a bad time of it, until I asked my sister Norah to help. And this was all right, because she needed to add some extra points or whatever it is to her Social Security standing, and I like any excuse to spend time with her. So she came almost every week, and patiently looked through a lot of piles of old printed and unpublished material about other places I'd made notes or written stories about. Gradually she pulled things together. I was of almost no help, because I felt a creeping distaste for the whole idea. I know now that this was because it was not *my* idea . . . I was doing it to order! This sounds egomaniacal, and I am not proud of it, but it is plainly so.

I thought the collection should be called *Places,* or perhaps *Other Places* or *More Places,* simply to make it clear that it consisted of short things not directly related to the subjects of the two other books. Then Judith said she did not like that. We fished around for another title. Perhaps it is my fault that the book took off in a new direction, because somewhat desperately I suggested *As They Were,* still thinking it would refer to *places,* and that was used.

But immediately I saw that it was no longer about places at all, but was being touted from the beginning as autobiographical memoirs and random personal chitchat. I was shocked-hurt-ashamed-resentful as the book took on real speed. I felt like a cheat and a charlatan with every fan letter, every sickening review. Judith was blissful. My agent purred. I was gently urged to give interviews, and be photographed, and I felt swamped by all the mail, all the eager earnest bright journalists and cameramen to feed and smile at and sparkle for and be nice to.

Well . . . it's boring to detail, of course. Probably the worst part was the fan mail, because a lot of really fine kind intelligent people kept telling me that I had changed their lives, saved their reason or health . . . I had been their solace during childbirth and divorce and even grave deadly illnesses. I had comforted them; I had inspired them to keep on living, etc., etc.

While Norah was pulling the book about places together, and I was writing feeble little introductions and explanations and so on, she (and I, a little) pulled out of the piles of material a book about aging,* and easily another book took shape, and I felt fine about it, because it was mine and I could simply offer it and say, Take it if you want it. So I/we did, and it will be published next spring, and it will probably not sell very well but it will be my view of some things about aging, just as I think even the "idea book" about places could have been just that—an honest little unimportant collection about one subject—if it had not suddenly become *not* about places at all but a random wandering attempt at "autobiographical memoirs."

MURDER.

Well, I finally read John Updike's review of *As They Were* and saw that he too considered it a kind of mishmash of such reminiscences. But since he reviewed it after it was obviously considered "important" by too many people to ignore, he read it rather grudgingly as autobiographical. This was in a way the *coup de grâce* for me, because I admire him as a writer and only somewhat less so as a critic of modern prose. It appalled me that he *had* to read this unimportant and rather shoddy collection. It hurt my pride.

But I could not tell him that. So I thanked him for his kind review, and sealed the polite note, and went untroubled into sleep. I did not expect or even want a night thought.

But there it was, the bell with one silver peal catapulting me into great clarity, for a few seconds or minutes, in the darkest part of the night. I lay listening to the words. They soon grew tumbled and thickened, and there were more and more of them, but I hung on to the first message: that the reason I had felt an increasing anger and sickness was that I had sold out. I had consented to an

Sister Age, Alfred A. Knopf, 1983.

idea book, and to a changed intent and title and aim, and to a new and big and fat audience. It was not that the reviewers and the fans and the interviewers and the photographers were stupid dolts and dupes. I was the dupe and the dolt.

So, as the first clarity clouded over, I hung on to all I could of the night thought, and felt strong and healthy and infinitely relieved. And I still do, in a way that is of course even more obfuscated by now.

I'll never let this happen again. I'll take whatever money that may come in and spread it as best I can where it will help the human condition. I'll help if I can with the book about aging, but I will not give any more interviews and I will not take any more jobs and I will not pose for any more photographers unless I want to—which is probably never, although many of them are interesting people. I plan to catch up with badly neglected personal letters, and write, when and what I want to write, and perhaps get rid of a lot of old notes and papers and so on.

I know fan mail will continue to come in for a time, and I'll answer it. It is a humbling experience, and never again will I feel scornful and disgusted because people have been led to believe something that is dishonest. If they have read some old pieces about other places than Aix and Marseille and believe that they have read autobiography, they are not perforce dupes. They read material I wrote honestly, and if anyone got fooled, it was I and not they, since it was fobbed off to them in false colors.

As for night thoughts as such, it is plain that they can be lifesavers! Certainly they must always be listened to, and if possible kept close to their first silver clarity. But even muffled and perhaps distorted, they can save us all. I'm sure I'm not the only poor soul who has willy-nilly been catapulted from a far world into this one in the black of the night, to listen to a true appraisal.

—*Glen Ellen, California, 1983*

34

Syndrome

The word *syndrome* is high style now, and of course is used carelessly by media and plain people.

In *Webster's Third International Dictionary* a syndrome is a group of signals or signs typical of a disease, condition, disturbance, or a set of concurrent things.

Not long ago, in perhaps October of 1982, several deaths happened in Chicago because people took Tylenol that had been poisoned with strychnine. After that, a wave of such poisonings, in everything from coughdrops to canned food, was reported all over the country, and in spite of the admission of mass hysteria, it was known as copycat murder and was often referred to as the Tylenol Syndrome.

I listened to many reports on the air, and threw down the toilet a bottle of extra-strength Tylenol-codeine pills that I had bought in 1978. I had taken four of them, with no effect at all on arthritic pain, but had kept them in my "guest cabinet" in the bathroom in case anyone wanted an aspirin-type medication but could not tolerate aspirin itself. So I was in a very small way influenced by the news on the radio, and I felt a little foolish as I disposed of the worn-out useless pills that should have been tossed long ago.

This morning my friend Richard called, to say that he and Gene had brought me a little box of chocolates from a dinner they went to last night in honor of Michel Guérard, the currently famous chef who was lecturing at the California Culinary Academy. Richard would come by this afternoon, with a visiting friend.

He brought them, then, with a bottle of some wine I have not known about, and we had a pleasant chat and I thought as I often do of how generous and nice he and Gene are. After he and the friend left, I ate a late lunch, very good, of some leftover frittata and a little roasted chicken, and then I opened the elegant little box (three ounces, it said in French and English on the bottom). It was the ultimate in modern design and packaging, in gold and deep brown, with a plastic inside that exactly fitted each of the eight or ten small bonbons, one wrapped in gold foil. They were small and delicately shaped by machine into a shell, a crescent, a leaf, a square. Even the milk chocolate was rich and of high quality. The fillings were fresh and quite liquid, with subtle but unmistakable tastes of vanilla or mocha or, in one, kirsch, and I decided to *eat them all,* instead of saving them for two or three niggardly desserts.

They were rather hard to dislodge from their precisely shaped plastic bed, and finally I had to take the plastic out of the little box and tip it up. The fourth one, though, rose a little higher from its bed, and as I pulled it out with my fingernail, I saw that a V-shaped piece of the dark chocolate had been cut out of it and then fitted neatly back into place. As I lifted it up, the tiny door fell out.

I picked it up and fitted it back. How curious, I thought.

Then the Tylenol Syndrome took over, and without excitement I tipped the little firm bonbon again, and the door fell out. Inside was a white and fairly firm but still soft fondant. None of it stuck to the door, which had edges as neat as fine cabinetwork.

I felt absolutely no panic, but only curiosity. I wondered almost carelessly about who had cut the neat little V-shaped door, and why, and if anything had been laid on the white filling, or perhaps stirred into it with a tiny wooden pick or needle.

Then I put the whole candy into my mouth, and let it melt slowly on my warm tongue, and go down my throat. We'll see, I thought, and ate another and another, and finished the whole exotic little collection in the next half hour, as I read the day's mail. I thought without really thinking that I had either been poisoned or I had not, and that I would know within a few minutes or at latest by six hours. It was then almost 5:00, so by 11:00 I would be either dead or alive, I thought nonchalantly.

I lay down for more than an hour, as I like to do now when I have seen a lot of people and worked hard and done a lot of telephoning. (Marsha was here from 9:00 to 12:00 for typing, and then the Sandmans came down from the Hexagon house until about 1:30 to have some wine and talk before they leave for three months in Holland, and I made some calls and puttered in the kitchen until Richard came with his friends, so it was pleasant to lie down and half listen to the radio.) I thought now and then about how strange it was to be part of the syndrome, yet to feel so disinterested in it. At the same time I felt that perhaps I should report it, in case I died or started vomiting or or or . . .

When I got up, I began to feel rather unsteady and almost dizzy, and I wondered if I was indeed part of the game or if the chicken had been spoiled or if I needed to have a bowel movement —things like that, but no sign of fear like a rapidly beating heart or shortness of breath. Especially I did not worry about why anyone would take the trouble to make such a skillful little cut in a box of expensive bonbons. It would have been easy, I thought; there was no plastic or cellophane wrapping to "seal" the little gift, and anybody could have taken out one candy and opened its side and poisoned it and who would know? There was only one that was wrapped in obviously untouched gold foil, the one with a tiny raspberry in kirsch for a center. The box was kept closed with a thin elastic tie of gold thread that anyone could slip on and off. Over the bonbons on their fancy plastic bed was a handsome kind of padding of gold paper backed with cellophane, and this lifted on and off. Yes, it would have been very easy to tamper with any but the one wrapped candy and the two flat leaves of plain unfilled dark chocolate. The little place for the fourth candy, the one with the neat door cut into it, was still obvious to me by its shape. I remembered it. But why? Ah, that was part of the syndrome!

Now and then my feeling of unsteadiness got worse. Finally I went to the toilet for an unexpected bowel movement—unexpected at that time of day, I mean. Afterward I felt all right, with no more light-headedness to take note of. And by now, at 11:15, I feel alert, myself, observant, detached. Of course that little door may have been cut in order to place a long-working poison, one that perhaps will not affect anything for months or years. But why waste it on me, an old woman? I ask coolly. Was it meant for Richard or Gene (who brought it innocently to me as a souvenir of their meeting with the famous chef) and because of their friendship for me? Or was it meant for just anyone at all, by the same kind of sick mind that killed nine people haphazardly in Chicago last year —killing to kill, to rid the earth, to get even with the world? And if there was no poison, then why bother to cut the tiny precise little door, which could not possibly have been an accident in that elegant package of cushioned plastic and gold foil and cellophane.

I fear that nobody will ever know the answers, here or in

Chicago. Or anyplace. But the Tylenol Syndrome will be coiled somewhere in minds and hearts for a long time, and will come out in the strangest ways, for its own mad unsuspected reasons.

I wish I did not know this.

—*Glen Ellen, California, 1983*

35

Les Vendangeuses

It is mid-September, 1983, and after ten at night, and I must stop everything to write about *les vendangeuses*, because I realize that they are very strong in my emotions right now, to my great surprise.

They are a small blue coarse kind of daisy that grows copiously in the ditches and neglected woods of Burgundy, the Savoy, the Vaud, every place I have lived where there are vineyards. And when the grapes are ready to pick, these wildflowers come suddenly into full bloom. They are the grape maidens, the blue-eyed faithful girls in even the brown-eyed countries like the Ticino.

And my house is full of them, and for the first time in my life I realize that to me they are Timmy. They have his strong blue strength.

When I met Patty De Joia, "La Ciuca," she brought me a bunch of them, and apologized for their being weeds but too beautiful not to pick. And I said, Oh, *les vendangeuses*, and I told her about them, and she said that she had brought them from a gully on the way home from her great-uncle's ranch where she and her husband Jim had been picking and then pressing the grapes since early morning.

Since then she plants them, I think only for me. When they are cultivated they make many more of the same blue flowers, with more small leaves and on stronger stalks. But they remain a kind of weed.

So now they are in jars and vases. And Patty and Jim are picking grapes, and everywhere the vineyards are bursting with promise, and I realize for the first time that *les vendangeuses* are Timmy.

Perhaps it is because I am quite old by now, into my seventy-sixth year, but I know that I am completely alive sexually for this man who died more than forty years ago. I have no need for anyone now, and probably physically I might prove to be narrow and withered in my sexual parts, although I have not cared or investigated for a long time. But I feel passionately aware of Timmy, more so than for a long time, and it is because of my new awareness of these strong little weeds, *les vendangeuses,* and the waning winy year.

I have had a few strong, not disturbing, fantasies lately about love with Timmy. There has been no orgasm, mostly because I do not want one. But I know that I love him with a continuing deep passion that has never been stronger than it is now. Occasionally I feel deep regret that I was not more knowing of the various arts of lovemaking, so that perhaps in his last dreadful frustrated years I could have solaced him, and probably myself too, with more physical pleasure than we dared permit ourselves. This will always be a sadness to me. But I did not know whom to ask, and Timmy was too proud. (Yes, I think that was it.)

So, now I am an old woman and I think passionately but with

a partly cautious deliberate detachment of the man I love. I'll never lie again with him, and feel him within me, but I'm thankful that I still have the memory so strongly always, and that the little sturdy flowers have brought it again to me. Dreams and half-conscious stirrings of strong sexual awareness do not bother me at all, and all I can hope is that other people may know some of them too, as happily as I do. I have no desire to bring them to any culmination, perhaps because they have already been fulfilled to my full capacity. I do feel deeply sad that perhaps Timmy could have known some physical passion openly, in his last days of enforced impotency, but at least we were good lovers while we knew how to be, and he never doubted my undying love, as these flowers now tell me, so long after he first showed them to me.

—Glen Ellen, California, 1983

36

Reasons Behind
the Reasons

The reason I am not in bed, or at least readying myself for it at 10:16 tonight, is that I have decided to stay up a little longer. I have just finished a bowl of rather overspicy but excellent smoked turkey in a kind of mishmash of scallions, green pepper, and mushrooms. (The turkey was left over from lunch with the Kellys here, a long pleasant meal after they brought me home from Norah's in Jenner. She gave me the meat.)

We had the turkey because when we went to Jenner from here, last week, we left hastily due to storm warnings. We expected gusty dangerous winds, probable power outages, no water, no heat. We took along my battery-operated radio and a portable battery lamp in case the electricity failed. We also took my chafing dish, and extra bedding. And along the way we picked up food that could be eaten raw, as well as the precooked smoked turkey.

The reason we were both going to Jenner, a few days before Christmas, was that on the eighteenth or thereabouts, I almost stopped, and I went down to Sonoma to the hospital, for the second time in a week, to ask to be started again if possible. I think I was almost done for. Everything slowed down. It did not much matter if I fell flat or stood upright, breathed or did not bother to breathe. The first time I went to the hospital, I was in prolonged and strong fibrillation. This time I was simply worn out, perhaps. Anyway, I went from emergency to a room, and after perhaps twelve hours I felt like recovering some sort of life, and the doctors decided to give me B-12 in the buttocks, and folic acid three times a day, and a digoxin too, every other day, for two weeks. Norah was here when I came home from the hospital, and we turned our backs on Christmas packages half-wrapped, and headed for Jenner, where she awaited many family people and friends. I felt pushed around—not by her—but I knew it was the best present I could give her, to go along so that she would not fret about me here alone, as I'd wanted (and had hoped and planned) to be.

So today the Kellys brought me over from Jenner, with the radio, the extra blankets, all the unnecessary unused stuff, and some of the enormous smoked turkey.

And the real reason, the reason behind the one about staying up after supper instead of going to bed as I'd have liked to do some time ago—the *real* one—is that my bed is still stripped bare and must be made before I can get into it. And I started a sinkful of laundry that must be finished and hung up. But before I can use the shower to hang it on, I want to wash *myself* there. In other words, I must completely make my bed, and then take a good shower, since I have not really bathed for almost a week, and then do my laundry and hang it to dry, before I can go to bed as I wish I had done, simply and easily and speedily, at least two hours ago.

The reason I feel as if I not only want but need a proper bath is that at Norah's the one bathroom is very cold. Also, it does not have anything but a long narrow old-fashioned tub in it, and I have not taken a tub bath for about eleven or twelve years. I am unwilling—really I am *afraid*—to, because I am very clumsy and stiff with arthritis, and I know that I would be a fool to try to get in and out of a tub without close and sturdy help, which of course I do not have. And I hate cold bathrooms, especially in winter. (*Two* reasons!)

It is now 11:18, and I feel overfed and too tired to move. But in order to Go-To-Bed I must do the other things, which I shall start *now,* in order to pretend to be reasonable.

B ut before I left for the bedroom I remembered that I must poach six fillets of fresh fish before morning, and cut three loaves of sourdough bread in half and wrap them for freezing. I did this, and as I turned out the lights on a warm and fairly tidy kitchen, I remembered something else that must be done before 8:15 tomorrow morning: I must count and list and put out in the entry the laundry that should have been off two days ago. I'd asked Patty to do it, but she forgot until too late, so she will take it to Santa Rosa early tomorrow.

So by now it is almost 12:00, and the reason I am not in bed is that I've remembered a lot of the reasons for not being there. Perhaps I should try to be like a cat, and sleep when I feel like it. But who will make my bed? I would simply wrap my fur around me and find a soft pillow to fit me—I am a reasonable creature.

—*Glen Ellen, California, 1983*

37

New Year's Day

I meant to sleep at will this morning. Last night I went quietly about the house, moving and putting things away here and there, lighting candles, watching the fireplace blaze–die–rebirth to blaze, until about 4:00. By then I felt tottery, and did not take as long a shower as I'd planned, the almost ritualistic cleaning before the New Year. I went straight to bed, to sleep at will and whenever I could and would. The predawn world was silent.

At about 7:30 or so, Maya Angelou and Guy called from Winston-Salem. They were warm and loud. I smiled, and went into a pleasant dream or two. Then at 9:30 S. K. called: he and P. would stop by *soon!* I asked for an hour's grace, and then almost went to sleep again, and finally forced myself into a very unreasonable facsimile of a coherent old woman. When they came at precisely 10:26 I was out in the garage putting an empty gin bottle into the trash can. I had drawn my eyebrows and put on a little pale lipstick, but my white-striped hair was brushed and still free, and I wore a nice Mexican shirt (presented lately from J. P., cotton, bright orange and purple), and dark black pajama bottoms and dark red velvet slippers. *C'est-à-dire que j'étais à moitié habillée, à moitié en robe de nuit*—and half-awake, too.

S. and P. are very nice warm boring people, and I feel that they love me a little grudgingly. S.'s mother is the same: she is careful with me, perhaps because she did not understand her husband and suspects me of enjoying his overt teasing pretenses at sexuality when he would *never* have wanted to be anything but a faithful lover to her. He talked and boasted, and dutifully she did too, of his wild amorous goings-on, and I laughed at them and also at him and also at her, but there was never anything but shared mockery and amusement there. And now that the husband is dead, the wife wonders a little: how innocent and funny was it really? I sense a wondering in S., too. But this does not dog me at all. And P. is latently attracted to me, as I am to her. She is a direct passionate woman, perhaps deliberately "free" with her long beautiful braids of black hair, and her Greek face. She weaves for a living, and runs miles every day, and takes courses in weight lifting and aerobic dancing. But she stays beautiful too, and today I enjoyed her warm unplanned embrace. S. did too—he is a subtler son of his two parents.

So they drove away, and I lied to them saying that other people were coming. They are not, but they are: I wanted to be by myself.

I wanted to be alone, by myself, selfish and alone, on Christmas too. I planned for it. I even knew what records I would play, all day, as I emptied old baskets and drawers—cleaned out shelves piled with unfilled boxes, put old unworn clothes carefully into a carton for worn-carelessly unknown people . . . instead, I went out to Norah's from the hospital.

If I'd stayed here alone, she'd have worried about me but

been almost helpless if she'd felt I needed her, for she expected David and Cory and Clancy and Hazel and Matthew and Sean and Anne and Kenyon and Brenton, and of course Lida had asked Niki. So I went to Jenner. (It was my intangible gift to my devoted and highly respected and loved sibling.)

(Here an interruption, telephone, from a friend who wants to "drop by." I don't like to have people drop by, *ever,* and this is a special day. So he will come in tomorrow at 2:00, while Norah is here! He is a bore, but she will help me with him.)

So for a week I stayed in Jenner. It was rigorous, but good. It made me think of the needs of others than myself and my wishes were unthought of. Now I push away selfish introspection.

Today is the second of delicious filtered sunshine, after too much odd rain. I can feel things stretching and smiling. (My handwriting grows worse. Ho hum. I am not used to watching over it. But today I want to stay away from the typewriter, the radio, the recorder. I want to listen and watch—light and dark and the shiftings thereof in this unfamiliar sunshine—and the sounds of fire ashes falling on the hearth—)

(Here I got up and put new fuel on the faltering fire. I am interested in how I am becoming clumsier lately. I fumble things and drop them. I am definitely slower in reacting to sudden stresses. Is it attention? Inattention? *Je-m'en-fichisme?* I suspect the last is very important in what is studied as old-age "deterioration": why *bother?*)

This morning, after the young people (P. and S. are perhaps in their late thirties and forties!) left, I did some cleaning in the bathroom, as a somewhat dogged proof that this is indeed New Year's Day. I got the storage cupboard for soaps, laxatives, hair-feet-body-bowels-eyes, etc., into ersatz order. It is ready for another year, perhaps. As always in such an operation, I found a few forgotten things like seven tubes of the Selgine toothpaste that

Norah and I got in Mouans-Sartout in about 1973. I tried some of the tubes and they are still soft, so I'll send half of them off to her.

Slowly I dressed for the day. It was almost noon. (I do everything very slowly now. This is part of the aging process, of course. I don't like being clumsy, but I don't much mind the slow getting out of chairs and all that. [Actually I *do*. I am bored by it. But what other way is there? If God himself blew a whistle, I would have to take my own slow time to rise to answer it.])

I've always wanted to try weaving my hair in a kind of controlled tousle on top of my head, the way it is left when I bend over and brush it toward the floor and then stand up. So today I am doing it. It feels good. The weight, if any, is on top, held up by seven gypsy combs—two red, two white, one blue, two yellow, in honor of La Unión in El Salvador. While I was pushing them in, I heard on the bathroom radio of increasing sorrows there. I can hear the bombs; I try not to think about the people.

I am wearing the Mexican shirt, so I put on purple pants and yellow-red canvas shoes. Then I put one long tinkly Chinese earring in my right ear, and in the other a shorter but still dangling one of cut steel, I think French Third Empire. It is fun, and I do not at all feel "in travesty" or pretending. I enjoy it. If anyone saw me this morning I would be sorry to have my privacy invaded but would not try to change my clothes.

As far as I can tell, the rest of today is clear. Now at 3:20 P.M., it is bright and mildly sunny outside. Part of me wants to go into my bedroom, lie down, perhaps sleep deeply for two to three hours. Part wants to stay here in the bright warm room to watch the fire for hours long, write to people about what they have given me so generously, sip some vermouth, and perhaps eat a piece of chocolate.

So at 3:33, I have tended the fire, eaten three pills and two chocolates, and decided to lie down. I hope nobody calls or comes—

And at 6:50, after a gentle snoozy afternoon, I feel rather "lost"—a little *dépaysée* perhaps: where am I and why, and what should I tackle next in this great pile of unopened packages and unanswered letters? I am aimless for a few more minutes. It was pleasant, in a stupid way, to lie passively under my pouf and ignore reality. Now I fight the return to it.

It is now 8:10, and I continue to feel rather listless and dull. I must do something, almost anything. The fire smolders slowly. I'll see what tomorrow holds—back here for M. V., I remember, a good omen of devotion to start another year. (I feel that I may not live this one out, at least as a whole person. I do not much care, except about how discreetly and without humiliation I can end it. In case I am meant to continue, I have several things to do. I'd like to do the library program on February 10, of course, and then perhaps go along with Andrew Hoyem's proposal to collaborate on a book with Helen Frankenthaler.)

Kennedy called. It was fine. Suddenly I feel almost alive again, and I'll go write a note or two. (Charlie wants some more supper.)

It is 10:25, and I have written to Jim Pollard and puttered here and there, opening presents, folding some of these back into their boxes to be given to others who may want or need them more than I do. (It is very hard to give "things" to people like me, I know. How would I know what to give to myself?) This morning: the beautiful afghan from P., and I don't want it. (That is, for *what?* I am already warm when I want to be, just as I can eat when I want or need to—there's an almost revolting *easiness* about caring for my current needs.)

I wonder how and when this first day of 1984 will end. I keep the fire alive, and plan almost subliminally tomorrow's lunch, tonight's supper, Charlie's breakfast, when to take two more rounds of pills. Gradually the house grows tidier, after too many abrupt changes in all my plans—two trips to the hospital and then the stay in Jenner, all in some eighteen days! I'll leave the Danish

Christmas bell on the front door until Twelfth Night, and the secretly amusing crèche in the far north window, but today I put away the two Christmas angels I always get out for beside the chimney, Anne Parrish's old colored lithographs that Tim liked. The house feels untidy but good.

Tomorrow P. S. is coming down from the Hexagon. She is bored and lonely, and suggests "helping" me with "something—anything." She has no conception of how I work, and of why I firmly said no when she told me she would write form letters, long or short, to all my fans! I'll be nice and so on. But she is impossible, except perhaps as a human being. (I mean that she is impossible as an assistant to me.)

M. V. will come before noon, I expect, as always. We'll eat, and I'll watch myself not to be teasing or exasperated by her. And at 2:00 R. N., who has met her, will come for a formal New Year call. Ah, yes. Ho hum. He and M. V. may have a little fine sparring. And I'll sit back and contemplate January 3—or 2, or 32—and meanwhile I wonder about the rest of 1. I still have almost one and a half hours of it.

And it is now well into tomorrow today—1:28 A.M., 2.i.84! Charlie is on my lap. I have done bits and pieces of tidying, and have eaten three pills and some toasted walnuts, and have read with enjoyment *Menu,* a New Orleans restaurant guide that I think I'll subscribe to. I'll pass this copy along to N. K. B.—it's well written, very "local." The fire is dying. I think I'll head for bed, after an artichoke and a shower. It's been an interesting up-and-down day. Why not? But first I'll look at a book I gave myself for Christmas, a collection of short stories by Colette. I expect to be envious, sad, bored, delighted in a detached way.

The next day, January 2: now I can finish yesterday in peace and well-being. The weather is brisk and bright, warm in the welcome sun. I feel fine and flush.

I went to bed somewhat after 2:00, and about 4:30 I took a pill "for pain" called Darvocet, I think, prescribed by Dr. Schantz. It did nothing to help the ugly gnawing around my new hip (metal does not feel pain, I am told), but it made me feel doped and soggy. I slept thickly until about 7:30 on my back, with my mouth open, unusual for me, and then rolled sluggishly onto my left side and reached for a mint to start my saliva again, and slept a good innocent sleep until the alarm rang at 8:00. And that's the end of the first day of 1984. It was good and bad. I shan't take another Darvocet. I'll not sleep often in the afternoon. I'll stay busy when I can, and sniff the breezes as long as there are any blowing my way—and try to understand what *really* happens in an hour, or a minute.

—*Glen Ellen, California, 1984*

38

Alarm Clock

A few months ago, or perhaps last year, I decided to buy an electric clock, so that when guests asked for an alarm in the morning, there would be one in the house—besides me, that is. I paid about fifteen dollars for a cheap but reputable Timex, a small white contraption made of plastic. It was guaranteed to be foolproof or drop-proof or something. I put it in its intricately designed Styrofoam box, and on a shelf in the hall cupboard.

Finally two young visitors, whom I'd lodged up at the Mammy Pleasant Ranch, asked if I had an alarm for them, and I felt almost jaunty when I reached easily for the clock. What a thoughtful hostess I was!

They returned it unused, the next morning: there had been one in their bedroom, but they were awake before it went off. So my little box stayed virginal until a couple of months ago, when for some reason I forget, I connected it to the outlet at the head of my bed, and set it on the shelf there. I think I had decided that it was foolish to spend several wakeful hours before an important hour when I *must* get up.

I use it often, by now, and I dislike it intensely. Its sound is artfully angry, full of exasperation and generally ugly abusive non-talk, like any sigh or whimper or sob or shriek, but purely *furious* without sadness or pain. It is a loud rapid rattle, snakelike but higher than an animate sound. It is man-made, like the voice of a computer I suppose, a mechanical imitation, so that even the shock it always evokes in me seems inhuman, nonanimal.

I have actually come to fear it. It hurts me. I would rather hear a real rattlesnake, even at the head of my bed. I plan ways to avoid it. I have foiled it, and on a morning when it does not sound I awake with a small feeling of triumph that once more I have got out of depending on it. I push in the little knob on its back a few seconds before it will buzz, and I am free again.

This sounds pretty silly, I know. Why don't I give it away, or put it back in the hall cupboard for an occasional visitor? (I think there have been only three or four people in my whole life who have asked if I had an alarm clock . . .) I leave it at the head of my bed, on my bookshelf, and perhaps twice a week now I tell myself that tomorrow morning I must get up by 6:30, and I remember at night to pull out the little knob.

At first I was clumsy about reaching for the clock, once the horrible rattle started, to turn it off, before finding the light button and sitting up in bed and so on. Soon I realized that this was foolish, since it was too easy to lie back, once I had stopped the sound, and let my ears rest themselves from its shock—and almost surely drift back into sleep. Instead, I soon found that the only way to take advantage of its nastiness was to leap out of bed and *then* reach for the knob, so that the warm spell was broken and any return to it was impossible, until perhaps the next morning.

Unfortunately I found a new trick, lately, that I knew at once

I must try never to play again. If by accident I push the little clock onto its back, the knob is pressed in, and the sound stops at once, and only my clumsy arm is out of the warmth, so that I have barely moved from my comfortable position in bed! No, I said firmly. If I am going to give this goddamned piece of machinery a decent chance, I must be fair to it. No more tricks, I said. If you are such a coward about that sound, either don't pull out the little knob at night and trust to luck, or be strong and wait for it to be there when you have chosen to use it. But stop cheating, I said.

And that is the way things are, today. I never turn it on at night unless I am ready either to awaken before it sounds, and get up and turn it off while I am upright on my two feet, *or* to lie in bed and turn it off as quickly as I can find it in the dark and then throw back the covers at once and be forced to hurry toward the warm bathroom. I think that I have compromised with its really brutal usefulness, and that I can let myself take exactly what I want from it and not let it disturb me enough to reject it completely.

—*Glen Ellen, California, 1984*

39

Beware

It may well be that spite and anger and even vituperation keep people alive longer than they should live.

Just now I looked at myself in the mirror for a fleeting halfway glance as I moved from one part of the bathroom to another, and I saw that my face looked hollow-eyed, with new little sags in the cheeks and deeper pouches and wattles, and a grayish tone, all over, and I realized that I might live a long time yet behind that changing mask.

I felt a new surge of the small and large annoyances and pettish furies that have passed through me lately, each leaving its slimy residue of plain *peevishness,* and I wondered if this was to be my bread and butter for the next weeks or years. God, I said, I hope not. I hate being angry and cross and peeved, and perhaps most I hate the egocentricity of feeling hurt and misunderstood.

It is all a form of self-pity, I said.

I thought of a famous old writer I admire. She has always

been angry, but she is not being so the way I want her to. She bickers and makes public quarrels in letters to the editor of big papers, and in general is an old bore and a figure of mockery, and I hate that and wish she would die so that she could stop it. But for a time now she will gain new life from every picayune quarrel she picks with critics or writers. She will turn uglier, and make more of a fool of herself. And yet she has such a brilliantly ferocious mind, inside that tottering old carcass, that she cannot be ignored. She is caught.

I am somewhat younger, on the calendar, but we both look like very worn old people, and we are both caught—in physical pains and demands that irk and nag at us—so that I know why she hates where she is. As I did, certainly, when I saw myself *her*. There I was, a harried tired old woman finding myself angry when instead I should be sweet-browed and tranquil!

Lately, after much thought and inner searching, I have written a letter chiding a good friend for abusing her right to use my name on a couple of recipes that were plainly adapted from mine and called mine, but *not* mine. And I have been less kind, but still thoughtful, to an interviewer who overstepped his position here as my guest at a meal, after his formal work was over, and printed conversation that had nothing to do with his professional reasons for coming here.

Peevish nothings like that I do not like. Neither do I like my increasing annoyance at the U.S. Postal Service for failing to deliver mail (most of it sent book postage and not first class). I am irked. I am frustrated. I do not know where to start any possible reforms, and meanwhile I learn from many letters that my packages and bundles do not ever arrive. This adds to my revivifying relentless *zap* of adrenaline, I suppose.

Certainly I do not want to end my days as a sweet-faced old Mom voted Dearest Citizen of the Year in her Hometown. But I can't stand the prospect of surviving on pure venom, into a haggard infamous death mentioned in all the obits with a sigh of earned relief.

I know just enough about glands to understand that we survive because of them, through what our genes gave us and what our lives have done to these gifts. In my own case I find it increasingly hard to believe that my dubiously good life must now be prolonged by my bile, my weltschmerz. The weary sad mask I saw tonight as it flashed past me in the dim bathroom was a message to me: *Beware*.

I would like to stop being frustrated by the loss of packages, and I wish people who are trying to write honestly would respect the common laws of journalistic discretion. I also wish that the plumber, who said he would come by the twentieth when I called him on the third, would perhaps come by the thirtieth.

But the main thing that makes me wish my face looked *nicer* . . . softer, calmer, gentler . . . is the vain and useless realization that it never can. My present small angers at the postal service and the local plumber and even my fellow toilers in the so-called media cannot alter the gradual settling of my nerves and tissues. My only recourse is to ignore anger as a poison, to reject it.

I decided to do that about ten minutes ago, knowing that it need have nothing to do with prolonging my own life, much less shaping my inner face and the time left to live behind it. Of course I don't expect anything to change visually, although it is possible that my life may be shortened by this decision if what I suspect about glands is correct—that I could live a lot longer if I stayed mad-as-hell about anything at all.

Lately I have been wasting a lot of time, waking harshly into pained awareness of where the moon is in the sky, with phrases and even paragraphs ringing in my dream-brain-mind-machine, complete with commas and periods, because I am a careful writer, even asleep. And the sentences were good. They were well and perhaps truly spoken, but they were also cruel, cutting, potent, death-possible. My mind was racing, my body warm, my breathing short and deep. It was a glandular and probably sensual gratification, no matter how unrecognized.

Perhaps this helped make my face harder and thinner. I cannot know, but now I have finished with this side of it. I am sure that my conversion, my being "born again," will have no effect on anything but perhaps my longevity. Indeed, my new state of blessed relief, this decision to stop being *peeved,* will almost surely pass unnoticed, since I have no familiars and do not care to mention it to anyone. It may even be thought that I have become a little dotty! Where is my old cynicism, sarcasm, bite? Where is my writer's heart?

I know that the mask of a tired old woman will not grow nicer. But I think that I may sleep better until I die, because tonight I stopped feeling peevish at fate, or whatever it is.

—Glen Ellen, California, 1984

40

Winding Down

It used to be called Aging, or the Aging Process if one was more discreet in speech and wording. It meant *getting old,* or *growing older.*

What it amounts to, in my mind at least and about midway in my seventy-seventh year (I was born July 3, 1908, and this is January 23, 1984, for computer's sake), is that I seem almost unconsciously, or perhaps only will-nilly, to be winding down. It is like being a wound clock: I have the original mechanism, but the ticking is slower, and some of the intricate tiny artful gears have worn down with long usage, so that now and then the ticking may falter. (This is known in some circles as *attrition.*)

I notice, and have done so for some time, a slowing and faultier rhythm in my walk, my speech now and then, and lately my daily routine. For instance, today I meant to have the bimonthly laundry ready. I got up early, stripped the bed and pillows, brought fresh linen, got out the old laundry in its basket and added to it from bathroom and kitchen. I put the lapboard with its usual folded paper on top of the used linens, and got a pin out so that I could attach it as usual to the bag. I planned to do this at noon, after my typist left—which she did at precisely 11:55.

It was then that the bookkeeper called: she would be here at 1:00 instead of 4:00, because her new baby was awake then.

So, at 3:44 P.M. the laundry man has come, leaving his bundle of clean linens but taking none away, so that I'll have to try to reach his outlet office about the next pickup. My bookkeeper has come and gone. I have not yet eaten the salad I meant to eat before she came. (It smells good.) I have fed Charlie, and am ready to eat, but the telephone has rung often and I have made two appointments for next month, and the fire is not yet laid and I have not given an extra-food watering to the plants on the two balconies and inside, as I meant to do yesterday. I have not located a check for $1,000 that I must send my agent, to whom it should have been sent in the first place. I have not written to dear neglected generous friends. I must send off some checks and cash others, and perhaps thank my stars that I can pay the bills. I must rest a little, this late afternoon, after some wilted lunch.

But I know that this compulsive attempt to stay upright, as Rudyard Kipling might have put it, is futile. I am winding down. I don't protest the process, because it is inevitable. I regret it because I wish I had more time to observe its progress and perhaps comment on it. That is plainly not meant to be.

So I'll eat some tired salad and take a little nap, and wind down some more. Perhaps the laundry man will call, to remind me of the neglected rendezvous with dirty linens—

But how long can this last?

—*Glen Ellen, California, 1984*

41

Journeys

Why is it that some people refuse, or are unwilling, to go back to a place where once they have been happy? If you ask them, they will say that they do not want to spoil a beautiful memory, or that nothing can ever be the same. (A wonderful thing can only happen once!)

Perhaps they believe that they are being kind and complimentary, thus to imply a perfection that must remain unflawed. Actually I think they may feel afraid that they will be disillusioned, if indeed they have had to convince themselves that a privately dull or ugly event was indeed a glamorous one. Or they may suspect that they are less attractive than they wanted to be, or that the other people are.

This has puzzled me since I was twenty-one years old and first married.

My husband and I went from Dijon in Burgundy, where we were students, down to the fishing village of Cassis for Christmas.

I lived in a mist of clumsy passion and ignorant naive wonderment, and although I cannot remember a single word we spoke, almost everything else rings like crystal in my memory: midnight mass, with fishermen playing wild sad songs on oddly shaped *hautbois* and windy flutes, over the bleating of two sheep by the altar glittering with candles; a new human baby wailing in its modern cradle trimmed with blue satin bows, and filled with Christmas straw; all the short square women dressed in black, with shawls over their heads. We felt shy and bedazzled, later in the bright hall of the Hôtel Lieutard, when the villagers gave us thick glasses of a sweet brownish *vin cuit* and everyone talked a very fast dialect as if we understood it well, and finally kissed us and cheered as we went up to bed. And ten thousand other happenings that are yesterday and tomorrow for me.

Of course I never thought of anything but a long full life with my love, but a heavy foreboding hit me about two years into this planned bliss, when he said firmly that we must never go back to the fishing village where we had spent our first Christmas. And a cruel mixture of disbelief and sadness filled me as I came to understand how thoroughly and firmly he stood by his conviction, that if people know real happiness anywhere, they must never expect to find it there again.

I did not like to argue, then or ever, but I did want to find out why, and his basic answer was that it was foolish to try to recapture happiness. When I told him that I honestly did not have the faintest wish to be the ninny of two Christmases ago, to "recapture" anything, he was deeply hurt, feeling that I had considered him a fitting partner in our ingenuous love, a fellow fool. Plainly I was out of my depth; I fumbled along about how beautiful the wild hills were, back of Cassis, and how good the wine was, and how much I had learned since then. It would be wonderful to see it with older eyes, I said. Impossible, he said in a pitying way, as if I could never understand the pain of being a truly sensitive poet driven forever from his former paradises by crass realism.

So that year we went to Nuremberg, and the next year Strasbourg, but we never returned to any place we had been before, because once, according to his private calendar, we had been there. And in a few more years we parted. You might say that we ran out of places . . .

I remain astonished, and very puzzled. It was obviously impossible to find out why he felt as he did, or to understand it, because I did not, and I still don't. When I tried to tell him that I did not want to "go back," it hurt him that I had not recognized the bliss he had tried to give me. And when I said that of course we were not the same as we had been, he thought I was telling him that he was older, which indeed we both were, and that I was unhappy that we were, which I certainly was not. And so on. Yes, impossible!

Fear may be a reason for refusing to admit change. And why would anyone be afraid of that? It is as inevitable as death, or "the ever-returning roses of the dawn," or curdled milk. And what reasonable human being would want to see always with the eyes of a bewildered lovesick timid child, which I was in 1929?

Many years after I was told by my young lover that we must never go back, my sister Norah and her three young boys and my two little girls and I walked over the high white-stone hills above the little fishing port of Cassis, and I cried out, "There it is, exactly as it was! Nothing has changed!" And we ran down toward its quays feeling delighted and happy.

True enough, wisteria hung richly from the trellises above the fishermen's doorways, and newly washed jerseys hung bright against the blue and green and white walls. Tough bleached old boats moved up and down gently on the flat indigo water, and down the quay there was the sound of a pianola I remembered from some thirty years before. My heart pounded with delight, and I grabbed the hands of Johnnie and Anne. "It's all the same! It's exactly as I knew it would be," I babbled, and I gave a big happy whack to one of the old familiar rusted bollards that still stood like sturdy mushrooms along the quay.

And it was made of *papier mâché!* It tipped over like a matchbox and rolled off into the dirty bay, and my sister and the children watched while (as I was told often and gleefully for several more decades) my jaw dropped like a startled puppy's and I seemed to *stop*—stop breathing, stop being. And then we all began to laugh, which we still do whenever we think of that wonderful return to the real-fake-phony-true place.

Maurice Chevalier was remaking one of Pagnol's movies there, maybe *Fanny,* and the whole village was a set, as much like Marseille of many years before as it could be made, and everyone was in a high giddy fever of participation, with the mayor and the priest talking together in the striped sunlight of the main café terrace, with some of the stars and grips and other people laughing as much as we were, if for different reasons.

My sister knew about my lasting puzzlement at my first love's firm refusal to go anywhere that had been happy for him, and we talked about it as we watched our five kids melt into the little gangs of actors' and fishermen's children. We sat under the paper wisteria in front of a fake café at the edge of the main set, and watched Maurice or Marius or somebody get out of a very ancient limousine countless times, for the cameras. Every take looked perfect to us, and every time the old actor creaked pompously from the backseat and stepped out, we smiled at his skill and then waited for him to do it again.

And I doubt that either of us had ever felt much more contented, serene, reassured. Quite aside from being well and with

our children and filled with various kinds of love, we were in
Cassis, exactly as we should be at that moment in history and
time. And Cassis was there as it had been for more than two
thousand years, and as it would be as long as there was a fjord-
filled coastline between Marseille and Toulon on the north shore
of the Mediterranean.

I think I was the first of our family to be there, between the
two World Wars, when my love and I went there in 1929. A young
fisherman rowed us far into some of the *calanques* to show us
where the homesick German sailors from the submarines lurking
there had climbed up the stony sides and painted their sweethearts'
names on the highest rocks: "HANS + ANNA," "Ich liebe
Huldi," "K. V. G." We ate the yolklike meat of sea urchins that
he reached down for in the still dark waters. It was so still that we
could hear a fish jump. We did not talk much, but the three of us
liked each other, and for several more days we could call and wave
and smile, along the three short quays of the village.

He might have been any of the older fishermen who stood
about now for the cameras so long later. They wore their grandfa-
thers' baggy pants and stocking caps instead of Levis and beat-up
visored baseball gear, and the children of Cassis were blissfully
arrogant as they strutted among the real movie kids and our envious five, in some designer's idea of how Marseille street brats
dressed when Panisse ran his pub. One or two little boys had tried
some makeup in their adventure as potential stars, and marked
freckles over the bridges of their noses, like some blond blue-eyed
urchin they had once seen in a Hollywood movie. They looked
touchingly improbable: dark-eyed descendants of the Greeks and
Saracens *never* freckle.

But they were part of our private return. They had been there
forever. And so had I. And I realized that the dear man who had
first gone there with me had never really been there at all.

Where had he been, then? We'd eaten and drunk and made love, listened to the wild sad rejoicings of the Christmas midnight mass together. Why did he fear to do it again with me?

Norah and I moved on down past the cameras and the serious village extras and the old actor getting in and out of his ancient car, and sat under the bamboo slats at the big café, and wondered. Lots of children came and went, and Mr. Chevalier came in alone and smiled tentatively at us, wondering why I looked almost like somebody from the Paramount lot in Hollywood a long time before. The white wine was cool and like delicate flint, as it had been even further years back. (Why had my love not wanted to taste it ever again, at least there and with me?)

Norah and I decided without words to stay by ourselves, and not smile back at the charming old actor, who looked suddenly lonely and wandered away. The children came along the quay with two American kids traveling with their movie parents, and several locals, still exhilarated by their professional debuts as extras. They were incredibly rich, at three dollars a day, even if their pay would go directly to their parents, but temporarily they were as broke as any proper thespians and consented graciously to drink a lemonade or two with us. The whole gaggle sat at the far end of the striped shade, like a scene from a child's version of *La Dolce Vita*. Norah and I looked remotely at them, and out into the afternoon shadows along the broad quays and the darkening water, and wondered how we could be anywhere but *there, then.*

I still think that first fine young man was mistaken. Perhaps his stubbornness was admirable, but his refusal to change his idée fixe was plain stupid, to my older wiser mind. Who wants always to look at a café or an altar or an oak tree with the first innocence and the limited understanding of a naive lovesick girl, or a homesick born-again Byron?

Five minutes or five centuries from now, we will see changeless realities with new eyes, and the sounds of sheep bleating and a new child's wail will be the same but heard through new ears. How can we pretend to be changeless, then? Why be afraid to recognize the baby in the straw, just because it is not as it once was, innocent, but is now tied about with nylon ribbon? Is it wrong to see the phony painted mushroom-bollard on the quay and accept it, as part of the whole strong song that keeps on singing there, in spite of wars and movies and the turtling on of time?

—*Glen Ellen, California, 1984*

42

Being Kind
to Oneself

This is December 26, 1984.

It is dark and rainy and without interruptions of people or telephones or anything more insistent than hunger and cleanliness and sleep. It is one of those special days, partly deliberate but still directed by unknown and probably beneficent powers.

Yesterday was a day of even more deliberate nonlaziness and no dawdling. I told all my strengths to be up and functioning by an early set hour, and they were. Of course this gave me extra confidence and/or self-satisfaction. And then I chugged along all day, until about 3:30, clearing off cluttered surfaces and in general preparing for an invited influx of assorted people.

The people came, in little waves, and by 10:00 I was gently puttering and putting glasses into the washer and folding the good old red-checked cloths from a couple of tables. I was thinking about some of the people. I felt fine. I went to bed by about 1:00, and instead of telling myself to be up-and-at-'em, I made sure that the alarm clock was not set.

Today I awoke with deliberate but very enjoyable slow ease, drifting into several little dozes after asking my other minds unimportant questions like how to use the word *it* or *go*. We played amusingly. I felt at ease with the Sub and the Un, which except on this annual day I treat with much more respect and circumspection.

Well, today, Lazy Day, it is now past 1:00 in the dark drippy fine afternoon and deliberately I have not gone anywhere but this room and the bathroom, where I have done two sets of laundry from yesterday. This seems rather significant, in a very minor way —the cleansing of the vessels and so on.

Charlie has told me gently, a few times, that he would like something to eat. I myself would like something, but right now I want to write about the possible skills and the general therapeutic effects of being *lazy*.

(My typing is not an indication of any values at all. Rather it is proof that I am less adept than I was even a few weeks ago. Not only do I reverse words, but the actual spelling depends largely on what keys I may hit. I feel sorry about this, because for many years the typewriter has helped me put on paper what I am trying to say, and lately I have almost given up using it because of my increasing clumsiness. I think that it is a combination of clumsiness and *je-m'en-fichisme*. As one gets toward the end of this current life, some things like remembering names and hitting keys seem much less important than they used to. This accounts for much of what is called loss of memory and so on in the Aging Process. It is really a kind of sorting out of what is IMPORTANT. The fumbling and forgetfulness and lack of interests are partly, at least, because of a what-the-hell attitude.)

So . . . on with my praise of being lazy!

But before that I think I should finally breach the gap, or whatever it may be, between the Other Room and food and drink for Charlie and me. First I'll check on his fresh water and food, and then I'll look twice at the icebox as I get out his salmon, and then I'll build a fire and then I'll probably eat something slowly and maybe look at a couple of unopened presents, and then I'll lie down for a quiet lazy listening to whatever is on KGO by my bed. It sounds delightful.

The telephone has not rung once today. How fine! Yesterday it rang perhaps thirty times, and then the doorbell rang a dozen or so times, and the whole day was a series of too-small crystals. I think there was a string to them all. Today I am not enclosed so far in any such lovely web or trap.

—*Glen Ellen, California, 1984*

 43

Games

I am now, as of about 2:00 on Sunday, January 13, 1985, going into a game with myself and also with Time, Space, and my friends and even people I dearly love. I feel both jaunty and scared foolish about doing it . . .

I've been talking for too long, several months, about finishing a somewhat amorphous but nagging "book."*

I went out to Norah's in July, and announced to my agent and a few relatives and friends that it would be done by Christmas. But in October I went out there again, to her welcoming and simpatico place, and I knew that the project would not be ready by the holidays. So of course I fudged along, because I honestly do not know if this hodgepodge of personal and arbitrarily organized stuff is any good. (That does not matter. What seems now to be important is that I do it, that I tie it up neatly, for myself anyway.)

* Her "secret project," this book.

I invited myself to go to Norah's tomorrow, and I told "people" that I would not be here until early in February, perhaps February 5. Then Norah said that the bottom floor was being painted and Lida would be sleeping in "my" room, the Think Tank. So I decided to keep to the plans and simply not tell anyone that I would indeed be here for a few more days. The thought of regearing my mind for cooking and being with both familiar and unknown people coming for lunch and supper, of marketing again and heating up the cold furnaces of my heart and mind—I decided *no*.

So I wrote to N. that instead of coming out after the paint smoke had settled, I would like to stay here, *secretly*. Everybody would think I was gone. A very few here would be in cahoots: Marsha, Norah herself, Kennedy, and of course the foreman at the ranch.

I have not heard yet from Norah. She may get my letter tomorrow. In it I asked her to call me: let the phone ring twice, hang up, and then ring again. Marsha tried this successfully.

It all seems odd to me. But the main thing is that I must try to establish, or reestablish, a different pattern of survival from the one I've let myself fall into. I believe and even fear that I feed upon the many people who come here. They not only give me an excuse for not facing my own work, but they give me a mental and moral challenge that is easier to me: I can be charming, thoughtful, attentive, the nice old writer belonging to her admirers. It is easier than putting myself and even my increasingly mussy and cluttered belongings into better order. I heap a few coals, here and there.

So at 9:00 tomorrow morning instead of fitting comfortably back into my old pattern of "Oh, do come to dinner, yes, yes, please do," I am going to pretend that I am on the way out to Jenner.

The road is familiar. I'll arrive, and after a good little drink, we'll have a delicious lunch, probably a pâté or some cracked crab and a salad. Then I'll unpack, lie down, snooze, pretend that I am really getting into a new skin, go out for a look at *M.A.S.H.* or something about 7:00 on the unaccustomed TV, eat a nice little supper, slouch off to bed . . . and the next morning I'll get up early and *start work*.

I do work well there. So why not here? It is a question of my own need to and my wish to, and I think they are both genuine. So . . .

I am indeed playing a game.

Today I am readying myself, so that instead of spending tomorrow getting into it, as I would at Jenner, I plan to start work at 9:00.

And instead of going out there at the end of the week, I'll be here. And instead of answering every ring of the telephone, I will wait for the code ring. This may be the hardest part for me, because when there is a telephone I listen. (In France I never heard one ring, in perhaps fifteen or so of the many years I lived there. But here I wonder if a child has fallen off a swing, or if Mother has had another heart attack, or if Father needs me at the office.)

And nobody will come for lunch or for anything. Everybody will think I am not here. I may feel very empty—never alone and probably not even lonely, but *away*. On Thursday Charmoon will come to go out for whatever I need to eat, and meanwhile I hope he will be able to hook up a new recorder-radio I've perhaps foolishly bought. And every day or so Marsha will come to get the mail and take it home for inspection—urgent, business, all that. She will call me using the code, as if I were at Norah's.

In other words, we are all playing a little silly game, because I want to try to order in my mind a book that may or may not please me. And if I don't like it, I'll scrap it. And if I do, I'll send it along to Bob Lescher and to Judith and to the *New Yorker*.

So now it's my turn. I've decided to play, and I am ready to —or so I like to think.

Actually I am very hungry, because I was about to eat lunch when the Freibergs came with oranges and so on, and then I felt that I must put this down before I stupefied myself with the good food that my innards want, even though I would much rather work here, right now, than eat. This will be another thing to cope with, during the next days. I often do not want to interrupt myself, but Norah and Lida have three meals a day, and I always join them for these. So for tomorrow I'll eat perforce about 1:00 and 7:30. All right.

It's my play.

—Glen Ellen, California, 1985

44

The Difference Between Dawdling and Waiting

Right now I think, or I thought so until a few minutes ago, that I am dawdling. I think (or thought) that this was because I am trying to cope with the odd chill fact that I can no longer write clearly in what we were taught to call "longhand" (pen or pencil in one's trained or undisciplined *hand*). It is not only difficult but tiring to try to keep even my signature legible. And what may be even harder to accept in both present and future is that my typing is even worse than my script.

I reverse letters (*nda* for "and"), which I've often done in the past. But now I not only write *tifleau* for "beautiful," but I am at times *unable* to write all the letters. It is as if I were rushing, too fast and busy.

This is clearly an advance in what is amiably called PD— Parkinson's disease. I am finding it almost too difficult (boring?), now and then, to accept. So I *dawdle*. I put off looking at the mail. I get out a recipe, but I wait until later to make it. (I even get out all the ingredients and put the recipe near them, and then I lie on my bed, under my warm soft pouf.)

This morning I asked myself when in the rest of my unnatural life I had dawdled. Perhaps when I was about fourteen, when I was a miserable human brat. Or perhaps when I was drifting arrogantly from one college to another, I coasted. I slept, or I cleaned all night, or I played tennis. But perhaps I was *not* dawdling (wasteful human lazy behavior). Perhaps I was *waiting*.

I was waiting to escape from being *entre deux âges* when I was fourteen. Later I was waiting to escape from my young life, which then meant losing my virginity and marrying into another physical and even mental world.

So now I understand that I am *not* dawdling. I am waiting. I am waiting to move on, which at my age means dying. I wonder about how best to do it, most neatly. I must now wait, to learn more.

—*Glen Ellen, California, 1985*

45

Leftovers

One reason that they are disdained is that usually they can never happen again. They can never taste the same, and good eaters do not wish to form any addictions that are hopeless from the start.

Another trouble with them is that their recipes are almost impossible to write. There is no way to capture again the taste of a cupful of yesterday's sautéed mushrooms put at the last minute into a spinach soup because two more people turned up for supper.

—Glen Ellen, California, 1985

46

Furniture

Looking across this room, I see a small rolltop, stand-up, veneered "secretary." I like it. It is lovingly restored, satiny with nutritive oils and waxes, a nice thing to feel friendly with. If I roll up the top, there are tiny nooks for inkwells, tiny drawers for pins or secret papers. There is a drawer underneath, copious enough. Below, two doors open on a place where the clerk may once have put his legs.

In other words, I like this artifact, and it is mine. It is in my current possession, partly because it belonged to my maternal grandfather, whom I met when I was an infant but do not remember. He asked my mother to give it to me, which I think was good of him. It was neglected for a long time, used to hold nails and screws in the tool room in the barn. Then Mother, who had a feeling for fine cabinetry as well as family, rescued it and had it restored, more or less, for my eighteenth birthday. I was not as impressed then as I was later.

By now I feel that I not only possess but love this tidy little piece of furniture. I am responsible for it. Where will it, where should it, find another home?

—Glen Ellen, California, 1985

47

Jumping from Bridges

Now I am thinking about jumping from the Golden Gate Bridge, and about other places where people have jumped to their deaths for many years. I think I should find out more about this, for I have an idea that there is some sort of collection of spirit strength or power or love in them that says *no,* or *yes,* or *now.*

I feel very strongly that this is true about the Golden Gate Bridge. Today, I heard that people are trying once more to build a kind of suicide-prevention railing along its side, which would keep us from seeing the bay and the beautiful view of the city. I haven't read much about suicide lately, but I believe that almost 98 percent of such deaths leave more evil than good after them. Even my husband Dillwyn's death, which I still feel was justified, left many of us with some bad things. And when my brother died, about a year after Timmy did, my mother asked me very seriously if I felt that Timmy's death had influenced David to commit his own suicide, which to me remains a selfish one, compared to the first. I said, "Of course, yes! I do think so, Mother." And I *did* think then that Timmy's doing away with himself helped my young brother David to kill himself, a year later. But there was *really* no connection; we don't know what the limit of tolerance is in any human being.

I do think, though, that there *has* to be a place where one can jump to one's death. There have always been such places. There is one in Japan that is quite famous. I believe it has something to do with beautiful Mount Fujiyama, which I saw in a strange breathtaking view from far away one day when Norah and I were in Japan in 1978. We had gone out with our chauffeur to meet some people for lunch, and suddenly the driver stopped the car abruptly. He said in an odd voice, "Look! Look!" And there, rising above a most dramatic Japanese-carved bank of mist and dark and light and lavender and white, was Fujiyama.

Even from a distance I could feel some of its enormous magic, and my hair prickled on my head. It was so beautiful! It was exactly like all the bad pictures I had seen on calendars and cans of beer. But it was *there,* and it was beautiful beyond the face of any god. It was all-powerful, and I felt like dying.

I have always known there are some people who must jump, but I never really knew about it myself until I was almost overcome once by a need to go off the Golden Gate Bridge. I feel quite impersonal about it now, just as I did the day Arnold Gingrich came out and dedicated one whole day to me.

He said, "Please, let's make a list of everything you like to plan but never really do." It was all very touristy: we went to the Cliff House first, and then we drove to the San Francisco end of the Golden Gate Bridge where I thought we would walk halfway across and then walk back. I never did tell Arnold about what happened, but about a quarter of a mile onto the bridge I realized that the whizzing cars on one side, and the peaceful bay on the other, were splitting me in two. The stronger half looked toward the city, the beautiful tranquil city, and I was almost overcome with the terrible need to jump off and be more peaceful.

I know it wasn't the sound of the traffic. It was a kind of force that was almost as strong as I, and I felt sick at the effort to resist it. I remember I took Arnold's arm and said, very coolly, "Let's go back now. Let's not go any further." And without any question we turned around, and I stayed on the inside track, near the bridge rail, and as long as I kept my hand firmly on Arnold's arm, I knew I would not do anything foolish. But I know too that I have never had such a strong feeling of forces outside myself, except once in Stonehenge—

No, now that is not exactly true; there *were* two or three other times. One, I remember, was on the steps of the cathedral in Dôle, a miserable little dim rainy city on the edge of Burgundy. I was standing on the steps of the cathedral when suddenly I was overcome by a feeling of evil. And instead of running into the church for holy reassurance, I ran away. I had to get away from the church, not into it. Maybe I could trace this back somehow to Carmina Burana and those secular plays that were given on the steps of the old cathedrals, like Dôle's. I don't know, but for a minute I was almost overcome by older spirits than mine.

And one time I felt a wave of horror, when Al and I were living in a room in Dijon above a pastry shop on the Rue Monge. I didn't know it then, but the little square where I went to get water in big pitchers for our cooking and washing and so on had been an execution spot during the French Revolution. The guillotine had been set up in that little *place,* and many fine Burgundians had had their heads roll there.

I remember our apartment was charming—one large room with three windows looking down onto the old *place.* It was big and airy with a red tiled floor and a little old fireplace; it had been a parlor, I'm sure, in a modest townhouse. There was an alcove with a bed in it, and Al slept on the outside of the bed and I was on the inside, and one night I jumped right over him and stood in the middle of the room, overcome by a sense of horror and fear. I felt filthy. Al woke up and asked me what was wrong. I said, "Nothing! Nothing!" But I felt absolutely clammy and horror-stricken by something I did not understand.

Such times have made me believe that there are congregations of evil and that they are stronger than any of us. This is why people who are perhaps weak to begin with jump to their deaths at times. Perhaps many of them, like me, do not want to jump off into the deep water far, far below, but something says: Get out! Jump!

This is why I have often said, in a rather casual way, that I don't think there should be a fence on the Golden Gate Bridge. Some people are going to jump. And if they can't join the waters deep below, and be swept out to sea—or, very rarely, picked up and made to survive the ordeal of hitting that surface so far below —I think there should be someplace else for them. But that place, and others like it, have always been chosen not by the citizens of San Francisco or elsewhere, and not by the people who built the bridge, but by something much stronger than we know about.

Perhaps there is something about water, or anything bridging a body of water, that seems to attract people to jump off out down into it. Very few people jump down into a pit of manure, except by accident, but there is something about a bridge over clear water, no matter how far down (perhaps the farther the better), that does pull people down into it, toward it. I know this pull well, and I have no feeling of impatience or anything but tolerance for the people who jump. There *must* be those places. There are those places.

I have not said that the Golden Gate itself had a feeling of evil when I almost jumped off it. Rather, I felt an urging toward oblivion, I suppose, toward peace. I do not believe it was bad. I do feel the Golden Gate Bridge is a place of great beauty, where many people merge with that beauty into a kind of serenity, a compulsion to get out of this world and into a better one. And that is not evil at all. But I do know that there are many evil things that lurk in the minds of the people who are left after the suicide of somebody they love.

—Glen Ellen, California, 1986

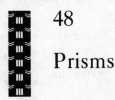

48
Prisms

When I went to school for the first time, at about seven years of age, my goddess had hung a prism in the eastern window of her room at the Penn Street School in Whittier, California.

Her name was Miss Newby, and the piece of simply cut glass cast mysterious colors here and there as the air currents and the seasons changed. It seemed a natural part of the new dimensions in my life. I watched the colors and wondered.

My little sister, two years younger, went to the first "kindergarten" (an odd Teutonic word when we were not even allowed to call the "liberty measles" German!), which was built in the basement at Penn Street School. This was fine—for me, anyway. I was told to hold Anne's hand the whole way from our house to school, about three blocks, with only one street (Philadelphia) to cross. I was to bring her home for lunch in the same tame-bear-with-clown position. I did so, aware always that she was in love with Andy on the boys' side of the fence that separated us then. I never told her about Miss Newby's prism.

By now I have one. It is not the same, of course. Hers flashed and danced all over the walls, when the sunlight was sloping into her big room in the winter months.

—Glen Ellen, California, 1986

49

White Wine Trips

I have no idea how or when my family started to take white wine trips, just as I don't know where our family jokes and teasings and names came from. Perhaps it was my mother and father who started them. I don't remember. I don't think we took them, calling them white wine trips, until perhaps we all drank wine. But we have certainly always had them since we grew up.

Father would say, "Is there any more wine?" or "Is there any more of this *white* wine?" It was *always* white wine, for some reason. And Mother, if she sensed a little argument in the air, or even if she didn't, would say, "I loathe arguments." "No, it is only a little discussion, Edith," we would say. But she would go into her room, which adjoined the dining room, always keeping the door open so that she heard everything we said, and sometimes we would hear her chuckling. In other words, she withdrew but kept an ear on everything, and we ignored her, but were all aware of her.

Father would say, "How about another bottle, Dote?"—or Sis, or whoever was nearest the kitchen. And then I or somebody would go out and get another bottle of very nice wine, and we would sit back for the trip.

It was always fun to seek ways and means of getting out of where we were into another world, or perhaps another language. I remember once when it was about midnight, Father said to me very sternly, "Dote, you go to the telephone and call the Mexican consul." I said, "Rex, I think he is probably in bed now." But he said, "Call the Mexican consul," as if I had not spoken. "Call the consul and tell him we want to have passage, and a house in Guadalajara ready by tomorrow morning. Tell him we want to engage a Mexican plane to take us straight to Guadalajara. We will go from there to Chapala or Ajijic. You call him." So of course I did.

I think Chuck and Nan Newton, my dear cousins, were there at the table. Sis was there, I'm sure, and Mother was in the next room. She knew we wouldn't go to Guadalajara. We all knew we would never go. Rex knew that the consul would not be there. I knew when I made the call that nobody would answer. But we all waited and I did make the call and nobody answered. I went back and said, "Rex, nobody answered." He said, "Well, goddamn! Well, let's go on. Let's plan anyway." So we all went to Mexico for the next two hours and had a marvelous time.

One time Father figured that if Al Fisher and I could come over on a twelve-passenger freighter from Marseille, then he could do the same. There had been no doctor on board, of course, and Rex would have needed one by then, but he said, "We'll take this cargo/passenger freighter and go through the canal, and go to France, and we'll live there for a year. We'll get off in Marseille, and go on up the Rhône awhile." We all had different ideas about where we would go. I remembered one Christmas that Al and I had spent in Cassis, and I said, "How about staying down on the

Côte?" And Rex said, "No, too many movie stars, too glamorous. We want to get *away*. We want to live like French people." I said, or somebody said (Nan, or maybe Chuck, or Sis, or whoever was there). "What if we don't speak by the end of the boat trip? What if we all hate each other?" And Rex said, "Absolutely not. That is impossible, because there is no place to go on a ship, and we have to take care of each other. The captain will be the doctor. He always is anyway, and the first mate and I will be friends and anyone who wants to can play bridge. And the crew . . ."

But we knew, as Rex did not know, that there are crews and there are crews. He thought that people took care of each other, and he was never much disabused of that idea—certainly not by us on a white wine trip.

I remember one time Rex and Norah and my two little girls and I were sitting at the table having a rather quiet white wine trip because Mother had died. I had decided to move to the Ranch from Bareacres because I knew I could not raise the two girls alone, and Rex needed me, and I needed Rex, and the girls needed Rex. We were sitting quietly talking at about ten o'clock, having a second bottle of good Chablis, and the dining room door swung open. There in the doorway stood my young number one nephew, the only one I had at that time, Sean Kelly, who was then about sixteen. He was going to a school in Palos Verdes and his roommate was Ricky Bercovici, who has since become Erik, a good producer-director, and who is still, I think, Sean's best friend.

Ricky was quite a bit shorter than Sean, who was then about six-foot-four. These two boys of sixteen were dressed in long black heavy coats down to the floor, and their faces were pale and their eyes were a little bit too bright. They both had on black felt hats, and their hands were deep in their pockets. Rex said, "Good evening, gentlemen, do come in. We're having a little trip here. We're having a white wine trip."

Ricky and Sean didn't smile. They came into the room, went

to the end in back of Rex, and stopped at the sideboard. Rex swung his chair around, as we all did, but neither of the boys smiled or spoke or even acknowledged us; they just looked intensely aloof. Father sat without a word, and we all sipped our wine and watched as Ricky took out oranges from every pocket in his long black overcoat, until there were twelve of them. And then he started juggling!

Our jaws dropped. Ricky was a wonderful juggler; I learned later that his worried mother had been told that he should juggle to keep his mind off his other jugglings, both mental and physical. He juggled at least twelve oranges in the air, and when he was finished they all fell back into the right pockets, which Sean had opened. The two of them then turned and walked out of the room and out the kitchen door. They never spoke a word. But they didn't seem rude; it was as though they were apparitions.

When they were gone, Father swung his chair around and we all took a big sip of white wine. "Now *that* was a white wine trip!" he said, and indeed it was.

—Glen Ellen, California, 1986

50
Sleep

I know that sleep is a gentle thing. It falls like dew and all that, but I have often wondered why it is so important to people to feel that they can sleep eight hours without turning over, or eight hours the minute their heads hit the pillow, or eight hours without a dream. All this has always been silly to me.

What is even worse, people often automatically take pills to help them get into this deep forgetfulness—forgetfulness of the day before, of what lies ahead . . . to my mind, it's a form of small suicide. Instead, I have tried always to keep dreaming, and apparently I do.

I'm thinking now of a favorite nondream: when I was a child, Mother always laughed and teased Aunt Petey, who traveled back and forth to Michigan a lot with her husband Moe. Each night of her life, Petey took one sleeping pill, and she always slept heavily, or well, or at least fully. One time, in about 1938, they decided to be really giddy and take a newfangled night flight from Los Angeles to Chicago, which then took about eight hours (a nonstop night flight with beds for first class, of course, and a stateroom). While they waited for takeoff, with Uncle Moe in the bar lounge, Aunt Petey did her hair as usual in their elegant quarters.

She always had it almost lacquered before she left for Chicago, so that she wouldn't have to comb it until she got there. She put a net over her stiffened coiffure and got into her negligee in case there was a wreck and she had to bail out. And then she swallowed her usual sleeping pill and got into her little bed and went soundly to sleep, as she had done for perhaps forty years. Eight hours later she woke up to find that the plane had never left the ground because there was something wrong with the engine. So it was the next morning, and there was Aunt Petey still in Burbank. And that was a favorite family legend.

My sister Anne, who took a lot of pills all her life, urged me once just after Timmy died to use one. She said, "Dote, you *must* get some sleep." I don't know why she assumed I had not. Perhaps she had not been sleeping well herself and thought that most other people were not either. Her remedy was a pill, always. I did not need or want one, but I took a Seconal, or two perhaps, because she insisted. She got rather hysterical, as I remember, about helping me in my grief, and I shrugged and tried to help her. (Sisters!)

I had a ghastly, horrible dream. In it I was aware of everything going on around me, but I could not get up because I was tied tightly by invisible cords to a log or a hard bed. I fought this. I think I fought it most of the night—a long, long time, anyway. And when finally daylight came, I felt that I had not really closed my eyes. I knew by then that I was not lashed to a straight surface, but that I was indeed lying on my couch on the porch at Bareacres.

I never told Anne about the bad time, but that was the first sleeping pill I ever took, and I wish it had been the last.

Then, in 1942, about a year or so after Timmy died, I went to the hospital to get rid of some little growths on an ovary. The anesthesiologist came to my room the night before the operation to talk to me about what she was going to give me. My one fear, I told her truthfully, was that I would feel, during the operation, the same panicky inability to escape from being strapped to something, held down, not able to get free, and to know all along that I was dreaming and yet suffering badly. She assured me that I would not —and indeed I did not. She did not let me!

The nearest I ever felt to that strange nightmarish thing after Anne's pill was much later, when I was in the Sonoma Hospital recovery room for several days after I'd had an emergency abdominal operation to let escape a tiny animal that had been biting hungrily at my innards. People thought I was dying of sudden cancer. But no. A little love knot had tied itself in my small gut, around the incision made when I had been in the hospital long before and had had my conversation with the anesthesiologist. This time it was 1978, and I was completely helpless. Tubes came out of me in every direction. I was pinned and tied to the bed, and all around me in the recovery section was the nightmare: everybody there was evil, basically *evil*. I was convinced of that.

Good people would come to the desk near my glass-walled cell to talk: paramedics, doctors, and one rather fat nurse who was pregnant. I had seen her before when I was conscious and not filled with Demerol and all the anesthetics. She was *very* pregnant, and she had lumbered to the desk just outside my door to tell the nurses on duty that she was saying good-bye for a while. They had laughed and made a lot of slightly crude jokes about motherhood, and she'd said, "Oh, hell, it's the fourth one and I said to him the *last*," and so on. It was all nice, in a chatty friendly way. But gradually, as my recovery went on and things became more and more nightmarish, I could see that what was really going on in that hospital was quite different from what everybody around us, all the stupid doctors and nurses, thought and accepted. They *did not know!* They could not know what I knew and saw and heard.

My fantasies were truly horrible. I cannot understand where they came from, because never in my life, as far as I know, had I ever seen or thought or heard some of the things I honestly believed I heard and saw and smelled, there and then. The pregnant nurse was not at home, for instance: she lay dead in a room around the corner from the big desk, her fetus lay between her legs!

As for me, I have been told by my sister Norah and my daughter Kennedy, who came several times to peek at me through the glass window, that my eyes were alive and peaceful all during this time. But I do not remember that at all.

Then one old-old nurse came in to braid my hair, and I thought, Next they'll wash my feet! Then they're going to carry me out. But before they do, I *must* tell *somebody* what is going on here, because it was becoming increasingly obvious to me that there was a terrible plot: first, to blow up the hospital, then to blow up Sonoma. And my duty, the only thing I could do in the world, was to warn somebody, to get everybody out of the building in time. I must escape from all my tubes, or perhaps I could simply drag them and all their squirting bottles down the hall and *out*.

Most of the plotters were the other patients in the dark cubicles around me, most of whom were dying. I know that several of them did die in the days I was there, and I thought, Well, they're just pretending. They want to lie here until they're sure everybody else in the hospital is really dead, and then they will come out and take over the world!

All this I knew was mad, yet I was in a panic to move, to run, to escape so that I could warn people to get the hell out of the hospital. But I was pinned to the bed, one hard plank, with the tubes thrust every which way into me.

Finally, I was taken to a private room, and I thought for two days that I was in the sanatorium at Angwin, where I had been before. So I asked a nurse where she had put all the religious books, because at the "San" there is a little shelf of them in every room—all the works of the founders of the sect of Seventh-Day Adventists, badly written tracts about how to die a true Christian, about how to live to be a true Christian. (Christians are Seventh-Day Adventists, of course, not Gentiles like the rest of us.)

The Gentile nurse in Sonoma looked at me oddly and said in a too-calm voice, "We took the books out." And I realized I was in another hospital where I had never been before.

When I first came to real consciousness, the head nurse came in and told me where all the buttons and things were, as if I were almost human. She said in a cold jolly way, "Now, we're going to keep an eye on you!" She showed me a little thing to press that rang a buzzer down at the main desk where she was. Then a voice was supposed to come on and ask, "What do you want, Mrs. Fisher?" And I would say what I wanted—"Pain!" or "Bedpan!" or something equally abrupt—and help would come. Then the nurse told me again she would keep an eye on all of us.

I pressed another button, as she told me to, and up in the corner of the room toward the ceiling a little crooked picture came on. She said, "We're keeping an eye on you, you see? So don't worry!"

I believed for several days that the picture really was an eye hidden somewhere behind the silly high screen that was keeping itself on me, as well as keeping its ears open. When I finally realized that I was looking at a small TV, I was simply back in the dream I had been having down in the recovery room. For Jonestown had just happened, and hundreds of people drank some sort of bottled pop at the command of their leader, a man named Jones, and died very quietly in an orderly mass, faces down. They did not die in pain; they just fell over dead. And here on the little screen were rows and rows of rather swollen bodies, all lying in the tent where they had passively, or with real resignation or fatality, watched their leader take his drink and die before them, and then they had died too, without question. (I believe a few knew of the plot and they escaped, or so I heard later. Anyway, it was a horrible nightmare then, and still is.)

So, there I was, pinned to the hospital bed, tubes coming out of every orifice in my body, and if there weren't an opening conveniently to hand, the doctors seemed to make another and another. And I was believing that I must keep the picture going day and night because my life depended on its keeping its TV eye on me.

All the news shots were of Jonestown, and the bodies, and of the leader as he died, or of the leader before he died. These tied in so clearly with my life of the past few days down in the recovery room that after a while I asked myself where I was—*there, again?*

Gradually I grew stronger, I suppose, and about the fourth day "upstairs" I told Norah, who had already heard me say some strange things, about the eye that was looking at me through the TV. She said that the eye really was an ear and that any time I buzzed, a voice would ask from the wall above my head, "Yes, Mrs. Fisher?"

We slowly got that straightened out. Then I said, "Noni, would you please tell the doctors that I'm hallucinating? I'm having terrible half-dreams, half-nightmares. I'm partly awake but not quite. They've got to change whatever they're giving me for pain."

Now, when people ask, "Are you allergic to anything?" I say, "Yes, Demerol." But they keep right on giving it if there is a need, which has only been once or twice since then.

But those terrorist dreams in Sonoma Hospital are the nearest I have ever come to feeling a hopeless inability to help people. They were the nearest thing to the feeling I'd had with that one sleeping pill I had taken from Sis. But this time it was *worse*, because the whole world was involved!

I finally did take another sleeping pill—to my amazement. I did not ask for it, and I did not want it, and I did not know I had taken it until it was too late to spit it out. This was just lately, the fourth night I was in the hospital with a dislocated hip. For three nights I had not slept because I was lying so immobilized that I didn't need to eat or sleep much. I suppose the anesthesia may have made me weak, but I never fretted about not sleeping because I'm made so that I do not twist around but can simply lie very still and breathe quietly and think about a lot of things and not let ordinary puzzlements bother me. I have many white nights—I suppose about one a week—and they never faze me at all, because since I was very young I have slept lightly. I have always liked to believe that someone might need me during the night.

But with the new hip, I had stayed awake three nights in a row, and unfortunately the nurses had peeked in on me every hour or so. They were appalled to find that all three nights I watched old movies; the late, late shows, the late, late, late shows—corny old movies, most of it terrible stuff. I kept the familiar old "eye" going because I did not want to listen to the people moaning, snoring, whining, coughing, dying. It is best not to *listen* in hospitals, anyway.

On the fourth and last night the nurses asked me if I wanted a sleeping pill, as they did every night. Or a pain pill. I said, "Oh, no." Then I thought, Well, why not? Tomorrow I escape, *this* time. And I said, "Perhaps one for pain."

But they gave me both before I could react, neither of which I needed or wanted, and I zonked off. I slept heavily. Hard. Without many dreams, I'm afraid, and for about six hours! I had not done that for a long time. I hated it. I really *hated* it! When I woke, I believed, although I knew it was wrong, that I had had my leg amputated. I suppose this went back to the fact that Timmy knew his leg had been amputated but believed, or *felt,* that he had a theoretical leg and foot. That leg almost killed him with pain, although it did not exist.

I was not in any pain, but I thought that there was no right leg there. How silly! I said, it should be the left leg, because Timmy's left leg was gone. And I thought, Well, we will match better! I do not know what I felt physically, but I was sure in my head that my leg was gone. I knew I was crazy, but still I told the young nurse who came in when I rang about my leg, "I do think that I should have been told! Somebody should have warned me about this—*discussed* it with me!"

I cannot remember what she said or did, except to hurry away. Another nurse came in and said, "You know what you need is a good piece of toast!" I thought of the limp horrible stuff they had been bringing up on the trays, and I said, "No, thank you very much," because I knew I was going home at one o'clock that day. I knew I had to get out of there while I was still able to. I also knew there was something wrong about my fantasies, because I saw as soon as I switched on the light above my bed that I did indeed have two legs! I could feel them both, and I moved my fingers up and down them lovingly.

(Of course, Timmy had always felt down his legs with his hands; he traced their outlines, because he knew anatomy so well. But after the amputation he did not seem to know that there was only one and kept on rubbing them both.)

The nurse came back with two slices of really good decent toast that had just been made in a toaster at the station a few doors down the hall, with sweet butter. She said, "I brought you some extra jam. Maybe sugar will help."

She obviously knew what was happening to me. And I ate every crumb. I think it was the first thing I had eaten since I had gotten there, and, of course, the sugar and the starch went to work and cleared my mind. But it was a truly scary experience, and I think, I pray, I hope I am going to make sure that this was the *last* time I will *ever* take a sleeping pill.

All I could think of as the nurse who had given me the toast wheeled me down the hall was Aunt Petey, all dressed and beautiful and her hair lacquered in place, waking up to find she was still on the ground in Burbank.

—*Glen Ellen, California, 1986*

51

Vomiting

People don't like to talk about it, the act itself, and I am not going to look up any definition of it, because everybody knows what it means. Most of us don't say the word. We say throw up, or upchuck, or or or . . . Once I knew two little children on a mostly empty transatlantic ship in January who told me solemnly that their mother was "doing wom-up all the time." And of course there are current phrases in all levels of education and culture and snobbism for this act of getting rid, through the throat, of a noxious something below it, in the esophagus or the stomach.

The stomach is of course the main thing, the real target and harbinger and recipient of no matter what we swallow. Probably the commonest poison we put into it is alcohol in liquid form. And when the stomach has had enough, it rejects its load and we throw up.

How we do it is a personal thing. I know people who can vomit as easily as they breathe. I have known others who can rid

themselves of this course or that of a banquet at will, so that in the
nearest ladies' lounge or facsimile they will get rid of this layer or
that of soup, fish, entrée, or dessert. (I was first aware of this
basically anorexic trick with an aunt who had a beautiful figure
until the day she died, like a dog, of cancer of the pancreas.)

Most so-called normal people are sick when they have abused
their bodies' tolerance. They get punished; slowly or suddenly they
feel awful, which means that they are dizzy, bewildered, with pale
sweaty skin and haggard eyes. Then they are helplessly caught in a
wave of nausea.

I don't feel like looking up that definition either, but it means
utter submission to an enveloping whirl of green-brown urging and
then helpless retching, and an enormous flood through the throat,
or in extreme punishment a thin bitter thread, from the outraged
stomach, where we seem to live and in this case to be dying.

Throwing up is an act that most of us know. I myself have
seldom done it. I honestly believe that I could count on perhaps
one hand but certainly less than two the times it has caught me.
But real vomiting, at least in my vocabulary, catches and indeed
makes helpless the people it has caught.

I never did like to look at it or think about it, which might be
of some interest to a Freudian but was a plain pain in the neck to
me when I was trying to grow up. I remember that once, in the
back of the car my father was driving up from Laguna on a late
Sunday afternoon, somewhere near Orange, on the road to Whittier, he slowed down and ahead of us another car pulled over to
the side of the road. Then a girl about my age leaned out of the
backseat of that car, and a spout of whitish liquid shot out of her
mouth like the water from a gargoyle on Nôtre-Dame, and I felt
sickish and horrid for years afterwards, when I remembered it.

But it was a waste of time to feel sick about it, and I am sorry
I did not tell myself so, or ask to be told so, sooner. People *have*

to throw up, to wom-up, to vomit. I would be better off, perhaps, if I did not have a prejudice against it.

One of my daughters can vomit easily, and indeed be almost unaware of the act. The first time she ever did this she was about two or so, already talking and of course walking, a beautiful dainty creature. I'd given her a little meal of half-frozen fresh applesauce with an egg stirred into it, because we lived in a hot part of the world and I had certain ideas about eating. She came into the kitchen in a few minutes and said in her precise way, which I did not then know was precocious, "Very interesting, what I have done. Please come and see. *Interesting,* Dotey."

So I followed this tiny creature, and she showed me proudly a very neat puddle of applesauce and egg, in a doorway. It was indeed interesting; she had needed to get rid of it quickly, and had done so and then reported it. And for probably the first time in my life I was able to clean up vomit without steeling myself to do it without adding to the mess—because I was laughing gently the whole time.

Many years later, I stuffed a big Christmas turkey with several dozen oysters, because I wanted to please the recently widowed husband of my sister Anne. I also wanted to please a friend, the new widow of my last and her last husband. (I was his fifth wife, and she was his sixth and last and best.) She too said she would like a big turkey filled with oysters, and my younger girl, the only child of this woman's sixth husband and me, thought a turkey stuffed with oysters would be nice. And his stepdaughter, my older girl, thought a fat stuffed turkey would be fine too.

I was in a stupor of housewifely motherly ex-wifely sisterly dedication, and not until later did I ask myself why nobody including me ever thought about the cold fact that I had lost *my* sister and *my* husband. So, late at night I stuffed the turkey with dozens of carefully seasoned and otherwise prepared oysters, and I put it out on the very cold back porch. (In hindsight, I knew better than to stuff a fowl before roasting it, but that night I wanted to have as much done as possible before the next day's duties called and so on.)

And during the night there was an abrupt weather change, and the temperature rose about thirty-nine degrees on the bird that should never have been stuffed anyway, and certainly not with oysters.

It smelled better than any bird ever smelled, and it looked handsome. The truth was that it was rotting. And everybody ate well of it, at an unaccustomed afternoon dinner. And then we sat by the fire, and then we walked about the town a little. And early in the night, as we all went rather soggy-happy to our beds, people began to feel sick. Not ill. *Sick,* in the English sense, which means "to vomit."

First my sister-in-law, my former husband's widow, asked our younger girl if there were any Tums in the house. I've always been stupidly prejudiced against Tums. I think they are for people who eat too much and then burp and swallow a Tums—people who are, that is, *stupid* about eating. So I was supercilious and unhelpful and rather bitchy about telling my girl that no, I'd never had Tums in the house and did not feel that my cooking needed them—that sort of thing. Hoity-toity.

I went to bed, up in the attic of the house in St. Helena. My younger girl would sleep up there with me. At the bottom of the stairway to the floor below, there was a little toilet-lavatory between my sister-in-law's temporary bedroom and my older girl's, where she slept with her young son next to the only real bathroom in the house. And in the basement below, where my brother-in-law was sleeping, was the toilet-shower.

And all night long the toilets kept flushing, and the people kept throwing up and purging their guts and then throwing up again—except for my daughter in the bedroom below (the one who could do it so easily). She simply leaned over in her otherwise untroubled sleep and heaved everything she had eaten onto a Chinese rug, which the next day her younger sister folded and took out into the side yard and hosed down.

The little grandson and I, who were either too young or too exhausted to eat the poisoned turkey, were not sick. My younger girl, the one who was in the attic with me, was too busy to be sick until late the next morning, because she was Miss Nightingale most of the time, alert before I was to the needs of our pale survivors.

In the morning I was aware that at least some of us had been very sick people. I kept samples of the vomit and the excrement in case the enfeebled wan victims died, and I was in my own hell of remorse and plain guilt when I called Dr. Neil about seven on Christmas, before sunrise.

I told him I thought that I had almost killed my family and gave him the immediate story and a brief report on the present condition of the three main patients. They were lax, chilly, weak, alive but only so-so. As I remember, he laughed, quite heartily, which annoyed the hell out of me in my state of fatigue and worry, and said to throw away all the samples I'd collected for the toxicologist, and to give the people weak tea and unbuttered toast when they asked for it.

Anticlimax. They did emerge from their vomitous states. They began to show some color in their gaunt faces. They nibbled at dry toast. My younger girl and I cleaned toilets, and kept the kettle boiling.

This is the end of the story about the Big Throw-up, except that my sister-in-law adjured me never to mention it, since it would look very strange to have international headlines about how a famous gastronomer almost killed off her family.

Why do I mention it? It is not a pretty act, nor a pleasant one as far as I myself know. I really hate to do it. Now and then I have wished I felt easier about it, or at least that it might be easier to do, but for me it is a major operation, a painful outrage. I think the only time I ever did it fairly neatly was before my older girl was born.

I was supposed to leave the house where I was hiding, by a certain date, but my child did not appear as scheduled, so Hal finally induced labor with a Japanese tea of savory. I had a biddy there to help me, one of his chosen retired nurses, and she was brushing my hair in front of the mirror, about an hour after he had broken the water sack in me, when I said with some embarrassment, "I think I am going to be sick."

She got a towel onto the dressing table and I neatly threw up onto it, without any feeling of nausea, and no ugly retching. It was rather like having a neat bowel movement, with no effort at all. The nurse took away the towel with its tidy little pile of vomit, and I did not even have to wipe my lips as she resumed her brushing.

The next time I had a child, everything was very different, because she came on Wednesday. But I do not remember throwing up. I hear that it is a normal way of easing the other functions of the body when everything is concentrated on the birthing.

I remember that before my mother was in a death struggle, she had to throw up, and now I am remembering too that one night when Father was trying to die he had to vomit, and managed to ask for a basin, and I got one. When he had heaved into it I showed it fleetingly to the doctor, and asked if I should throw it out, and he said yes. It had the black rotting lung of the man in it. It was horrible and part of my father, but I held it and then flushed it down the toilet with a deliberate coldness. Survival.

Vomiting is a good thing to do, many people tell me. By now I can contemplate it with deliberate impersonality, just as I can listen to a man with emphysema cough and spit out what is drowning him and not have my stomach turn over. I suppose it's a question of schooling.

But it still makes me feel like throwing up, if I could, to think about it without all the walls of self-protective reasoning. I hate the whole idea. I hate the muscular cramp that I have felt, the few times I have needed it, which forces the contents of my outraged stomach up through my throat and into the world. It is one thing to ready the body for birth, as I did, or for death as my parents had to. But the need to get rid of poisons, like rotting food or alcohol or something like heroin: that is another and uglier fact, and I accept it with an unconquerable aversion.

—Glen Ellen, California, 1987

52

Glory Hole

There is one word that I love, and that I use sometimes when I think of this book as I hope it will turn out to be, and that is glory hole.

It is, as far as I know, completely American, and I feel that I am one and that I write and talk as one.

When I was little, my mother often used the word (although she was basically an anglophile and spoke *English*). To all of us it meant a closet or cupboard where we put all kinds of cast-off and unused clothes, tools, pots, canning jars, rubber boots, aprons with one tie string missing, paper bags full of odd stockings, broken lamp shades . . .

Mother said that every house *must* have a glory hole. Now and then she would say, when we asked where last spring's roller skates were, "Go look in the glory hole, but don't knock down that sack of dried mushrooms!" Something like that.

And I've always had a glory hole, wherever I've lived since I grew up. In Switzerland it was a low attic, with woven strings of garlic and onions and shallots hanging under the roof tree, and ski poles and then backpacks lower down under the eaves, and cases of old manuscripts and a couple of broken cameras and other potential treasures on the dusty floor. But I had to leave all that before it really had a chance to be itself, because World War II came along.

Later, I lived in a little town north of San Francisco Bay for several decades, and the glory hole there was a small room, right off the front hall, that had once been the office of the doctor who had built our house in 1870. He had set legs and pulled teeth and delivered babies from there. It was a good little room, but gradually it became our glory hole, and a fine one too.

We had a big attic and a bigger basement in that house, but it was the doctor's office that seemed to pull all our lives and their leavings into focus: dolls to mend someday, and a broken Singer sewing machine, and parts of several projects my girls started and did not finish in grammar school—and a couple of unfinished novels.

One mysterious thing about a real glory hole is that there is always the knowledge, the belief, the feeling that sometime whatever is in it will turn up, and be infinitely useful and valuable.

Perhaps this is why I was interested to learn, only a few years ago, that a real glory hole is a place where miners in early California days kept ore that they suspected might be of great value. They would hide it in a glory hole, sure that someday they could come back and reap their just rewards from it.

Any good glory hole may hide an unsuspected bonus for somebody, sometime! And no doubt some such childlike faith in me, or some egocentric hope, wants this collection to turn up an unsuspected gem of perception or wit or down-to-earth amusement, under the dust and neglect that must collect in any such mental storage place.

—Glen Ellen, California, 1988

53

Potato Chips

Most of our vices are relatively harmless to other people, two- or four-legged—that is, I doubt that I taint more than my own liver when I happily, indeed voluptuously, tweak open a cellophane packet of salt-encrusted, preservatives-loaded, additives-flavored, crispy-crunchy, and machine-made potato chips. (They used to be called Saratoga chips, I think.)

It seems logical, or at least convenient in a somewhat jesuitical way, that I have earned this latter-day respite from my early dedication to the pursuit of The Perfect. I have tasted the best, I argue, and therefore am justified in solacing my last years with no matter how unreasonable facsimiles, since the best is unattainable.

It is unattainable here and now, anyway.

Occasionally, and always alone, I put some substitute for the Perfect Potato Chip in a little wooden bowl (this is all somewhat dubious and fetishistic from a Freudian or perhaps Jungian or even est-ian point of view) and eat it before lunch. (Never dinner or supper.)

The ersatz potato chips are not good.

—Glen Ellen, California, 1988

54

Quotations

One of the easiest ways to start a novel or an essay or even a conversation, if one is not quite sure how to, is to quote somebody else. Current politicians or movie stars or even authors can help, especially if they are notorious. And a copy of *Bartlett's Quotations* is always close by, or should be!

Once when I was both younger and more foolish than I now appear to be, I ran out of apt springboards in the middle of a book, and blandly invented not only a personage of some wit but even what he might have said to prove the main point of my next chapter. For several years after the book was published, to some critical success and only a minor financial deficit, I went on ignorantly believing that I had fooled all the people all that time. Of course I was caught out, by a cruel Italian psychiatrist and amateur gastronome whom I admired highly, and his mocking dismissal of my feeble trick still haunts me. He was very right, of course, to make my childish self-service ridiculous; I'd ascribed to some invented wit like Johann Sebastian Appelmuss a foolish remark I needed so that I could then say what I wanted to, protected by his infinitely more important mind! It was a farce, and justly laughed at, and I never did it again. (The Freudian Machiavelli forgave me.)

And by now I find that on some subjects there is so much I can say that even Bartlett is easy to ignore! My trouble now is not where to go for help but how to sort out one single facet to concentrate on.

—Glen Ellen, California, 1988

55

Frustration—I

I am in an unfamiliar but not frightening state of mind and body, and this note about it may be of some use or interest. (My typing is increasingly bad and quite boring to attempt as well as to correct.)

I feel rather detached and cheerful, mentally. My mind is clear, but not sparkling or witty. My mood is rather who-cares-ish, *je-m'en-fichiste*. Physically I am very slow. I walk slowly, and like to touch walls and furniture lightly all the time as I go from bed to toilet to kitchen. I do not like to build a fire, or get dressed, or even read. It is especially boring to cook and to eat, and if I were not aware that I'd be a fool to try it, I'd like never to eat again, just as I would prefer never to bother to pee or defecate. I'd like to lie on my bed under the covers in one unchanging place forever.

I think of Miss Eleanor, and how she gradually got into a fetal curve and simply dried up there, like a leaf. She was almost 102, and the day before she died, her daughter bought a water mattress that might keep the woman's old bones from poking through her flesh and making sores. It was never used. I'd like to remain like her, but the thought of waiting almost twenty more years appalls me.

I think that I have tapered off in perhaps the last three months, moving less certainly, especially in unfamiliar places like streets and stores. I feel unsteady, insecure, and prefer moving about in this small familiar house. This is partly because of the slow natural progress of both the arthritis and the Parkinson's. But the decline happened suddenly for me anyway, and there is no use either denying it or trying to tell anyone about it. Why bother?

A week and five days ago I fell, here, and I am still not well— a really shocking experience, although it actually did not bother or scare me. It could have happened at any time in my long life. I have always taken for granted that I was deft and that I moved lightly and easily and with good balance, and I forgot for one second that I am not as I've so long been, and I lost my balance in a very small space and had to fall against a sharp bookshelf corner instead of down onto the floor, as would have been wiser. I was counting laundry from the basket into the bag, sitting on the edge of my bed, and in one habitual and unconsidered motion I stood up with the empty basket in one hand and tried to push back the door to put the basket into its usual place behind it. But the door, for the first time I know of, stuck on the edge of the little rug I was standing on, and I was off balance and started to fall as I twisted around between the stuck door and my bed.

Of course the fall seemed to last a long time, and I knew that there was no space for straightening out. I went limp and limber, as I'd learned to do in gym at Occidental in 1927, and knew with real resignation that I had to hit the edge of the bookcase. I did so, and then lay for a minute or two, with the empty basket on top of me, waiting to breathe naturally. I felt no trouble at all, and moved to check out my bones and reflexes. I think I said something aloud, like "Quite a fall" or "Great one!" or something like that.

By the time I started to get up, which by now is something I arrange almost never to do, since I am stiff and creaky, I knew it had been more of a tumble than it had seemed to be. My breathing was heavy and slow.

I walked slowly toward the sink in the bathroom, perhaps six paces. I meant to stop there and look at myself for a minute and then go about eight or ten more steps to the toilet. Instead I lost control of my bowels, and to my astonishment, for this had never happened before to me, I felt my panties fill with a rush of soft warm excrement. I simply stood there, and looked at my astonished face in the mirror. Then I said, but silently, "This is something serious."

I pulled off my shoes, stockings, pants, panties onto a towel that I'd dropped under me when the inevitable thing started, and reached for another towel and wiped myself off, and folded everything into a neat little pile. I was breathing heavily. I went about five steps to the shelf for some toilet water and back to the sink, but I felt increasingly light-headed and knew that it had been a real fall indeed. I splashed the bath scent all over, and felt clean, and then went with great care to my bed. I knew I was in trouble. I pulled a shawl over my bareness from the waist down, and dialed the ranch foreman, and tried to remember other numbers. But Paul was there, miraculously.

I said, "This is Mary Frances. I think I've had a bad fall. Will you come down?"

Of course he came at once, and the room was full of four young Glen Ellen firemen in yellow rubber uniforms and then two paramedics and I was feeling worse all the time. Dr. Schantz was soon in emergency in Sonoma. There were a lot of very painful X-rays. I had a couple of bad chills, and the pain increased, but I knew that there would be no broken bones. And in three hours I was home. Norah was here for the night, and I got used to being a badly bruised old body.

The verdict was "significant bruises on right rear rib cage." There were other lesser and more visible bruises of course. They disappeared in a week. By now, almost two weeks past the horrid event, I can turn in bed and walk slowly, and in general move (with care) in a fairly normal way. For the first four days I took the maximum dosage of eight capsules of painkiller every twenty-four hours. I also took half a Valium for two nights. Then I took the capsules (a Tylenol-codeine prescription) only at night for about five nights. Last night I took only half a Valium.

Aside from steady discomfort in breathing and even ordinary moving, my main problem has been severe and rather peculiar constipation, a natural result of the medication and lack of motion, and also a lack of my average eating. (I have no interest at all in food, which was convenient when there was nobody around to bring it to me, but which is now my problem, and my embarrassment.) I seem to have it more or less under control, with a complicated routine of Effersyllium, milk of magnesia, and Surfak and even bowls of Raisin Bran flakes! It is repellent even to write about, and at the moment my bowels are somewhat too "loose." It was fine for about the first six days; I had absolutely no muscular obedience down there, so that I could not even fart! Fortunately, I suppose, my kidneys kept on working, but very little, so that I did not need to go often to the toilet.

Well—tonight I feel like an automaton, sitting here trying to hit this out for possible use by a friend or a doctor or or or . . . I really am very ready to stop going through the increasingly difficult motions of being an upright human person. I would like to lie down and not move again. I do not want to eat, or drink, ever again. I hate the thought that soon I must stand up carefully, turn slowly so that I do not stagger or trip, and walk into the other room and eat something and listen to the radio and then turn out the lights and come carefully and slowly in to undress and get into bed. What I want to do is go straight to my bed, and lie cautiously down between two small pillows I have fixed so that my ribs do not hurt, and pull up my cover and lie in the dark. I am not sleepy. But I am tired. I think it may be time for me to die. Why not?

But as long as I can, it seems, I'll go on undressing slowly and brushing my teeth and seeing that Charlie has fresh water and and and, before I lie down. As long as I can I'll try to walk to the toilet when I need to, without falling down or dribbling. And I'll eat something so that tomorrow my bowels may move and so that I can take pills as if I really cared whether or not there would be bad consequences if I didn't. In other words, I am conditioned to living as decently as possible while I have to. By now, it is a chore.

Charlie, the cat who lives here, wants something more, something different, some Oriental tidbit I have never given him. I go slowly toward the kitchen. Soon I'll go to bed, and it is more than likely that tomorrow I'll get up again.

—*Glen Ellen, California, 1988*

 56
Travel

It is seldom that anyone gets anything free that is very good, but the idea for this short statement was offered to me without any question of payment, so that all I can do is hope that what I say will be readable, which of course in my lexicon means *good*.

My friend said that "at eighty, the last thing you feel like doing is planning a journey." This of course is a complete refutation of that heinous conclusion.

It is true that I am in my eightieth year, which means that I will indeed be eighty. (I find that many people prefer to add or subtract a year or two in this silly way.) And the truth is that what my friend states is the *last* thing I should feel like doing is increasingly the *first* thing, as I add a little chronologically every day to my fairly full span of life.

In fact, I plan several journeys a day, and even more than that at night. This morning I went to a Mexican village I first lived in some fifty years ago. This was easily accomplished, of course, since

I was lying here in bed during the whole two years I spent there in Chapala!

Then, of course, I planned my second trip of the day, which took much more effort: I arose with extreme caution, reached for my cane, and with carefully measured steps went very slowly into the bathroom. There I performed my usual snaillike but always meticulous morning duties, and almost an hour later I was neat and tidy and feeling rather tired from this second long trip. And from then on it has been one journey after another.

A friend plans to buy a "perfect place" in Tuscany, of course on top of a hill and, of course, rather near Siena. So I went there with her, but not for much longer than to assure her that she must sign *nothing* without a local lawyer alongside. Then, I went quickly to Paris for about three days with another friend who has just come back from there. On the way home, we stopped in New York, since I would rather die than have to go through customs in Los Angeles ever again, as we would have had to do to get back to San Francisco. We went up to the Rainbow Room for a quick look at the new-old decor. It was fine, and the floor still revolved exactly as it had when I went there in 1937 to tea-dance to Paul Whiteman's orchestra. Then the phone rang, and while I was discussing going to a country club in Napa Valley in a few days, I was really in a small Swiss-Italian village with Romilda, who has just published a book in Napa about growing up in her native Ticinese (Swiss) village.

And I want to go over the hill from the Valley of the Moon to the Napa Country Club again, *not* to sign that silly book, much as I love it, but because I want to be once more in that little village.

Or perhaps on the way over the hill I may take another full-time journey and find myself in Athens. I have never been in Athens. Two of my friends are there this minute, though, and I don't see why I should not drop in on them. I might stay on, and learn enough modern Greek to read the newspaper every morning, and then go to a village on Crete and study the older tongue. I've always wanted to read Aristotle in the original language.

And all this is why I think it is incorrect that the last thing I want to do is plan another trip, simply because I'm not in my first foolish flush of youth.

Avanti!

—*Glen Ellen, California, 1988*

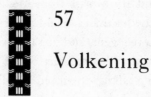

57

Volkening

One of the many reasons for my firm conviction that I am blessed, not only amongst women but just plain people of any sex at all, is that for some thirty-eight years Henry Volkening was what is too casually called my literary agent.

I met him because I'd just married Donald Friede, who unbeknownst to me had married me because he felt that he alone could change me from an unknown writer into a best-selling author. First in his scheme was to have me sever my pleasant relationship with Mary Leonard Pritchett, my genteel but successful agent. I was sad about this severance, which was done with more than the usual amount of misunderstanding and hurt and ill feeling and all that. Ho hum, indeed—and fortunately I could say this to Mary herself, many years after. She agreed thoroughly with me, so that we ended *her* days at least with a real and trusting friendship.

I was introduced to Henry Volkening early the first summer of my marriage to Donald, and by him of course. It was at a party given by Edita and Ira Morris from Mexico and Paris, both of whom I'd known better than Donald did. Henry was a small man, I remember, and a real gent, and he said a couple of nice things to me in an impersonal and somewhat bored way, and then I spent most of the evening talking to an old Swedish lady who sat cozily behind a pile of little cakes. I was shy, and liked the fact that she was nibbling and wanted me to sit with her and nibble too. Donald kept trying to make me stand up, and I realized that I was being gauche, and I don't think that I saw Henry again before we left.

He was definitely my agent, though, chosen and appointed by Donald, and by now this seems strange, because Henry was determined that I would never write a best-seller in my life. Of course, this was a great disappointment to Donald, but I don't think he really questioned the other man's motives or even his tactics, recognizing as only he would and could that Henry was a much better agent than he could ever be. That was one very fine thing about my third husband: he accepted and greatly respected people who knew more than he did about anything—about painting and writing, anyway. (In politics and other such Machiavellian pursuits, he knew without argument that he was tops.) He and Henry probably liked each other very much. Really, I *know* they did.

Myself, I don't remember anything at all about that first summer of my long good life with Henry. I was working hard on a kind of anthology that he no doubt handled for me, but I was apparently unaware of any directions he may have been giving me. Actually, I doubt that he did. Later on, he would chide me a bit, but rarely. I don't remember his ever saying anything in praise, although I'm sure that he would not have wasted his time on me if he had not thought me worth the occasional bother I'm sure I was to him.

Over the next thirty-eight years, he wrote many letters to me.

For a thousand reasons I regret bitterly that he never made a single copy of anything, nor did I keep one of his small closely typed pages. This casual way of running his own and his clients' lives made things difficult indeed when he died. In fact, they were a real mess, both after and before that sad day. His secretary Connie had no idea of exactly what he had written to anyone at all, and his partner Russell was in a permanent and furious fog about what and why and how Henry did his share of their business. Now and then Henry would write to me about somebody like Hannah Arendt, or Carson McCullers, as if I knew them closely, and probably he assumed that I did. He was pleased that I did know Jessamyn West, and I feel sure that he was disappointed that we were not closer friends. As for Eudora Welty, he seemed certain that I understood completely the hows and whys of his treatment of her, mainly because it was almost like his of me. He assured me once that she was both awkward and ugly as a girl and a middle-aged spinster, but that she would be a fine old lady as well as a great writer. I think he thought that although I was not quite as unattractive as she in my early years, I had less promise than she.

Still, Henry did his best to keep me from becoming the popular author that Donald had hoped I would be. And he hated my working for "women's magazines," especially doing easy monthly essays about potato salad and somesuch. Once he asked me why I continued to subject him to the female editors that seemed to be a part of any sheet I worked for, and I know that he was very happy indeed when I stopped supporting myself and the children by their monthly demands and wrote more often for magazines like the *New Yorker*.

Henry was cool about my earning anything at all, really. One year, I made $37.50. This pleased him enormously, and as he meticulously took out his own 10 percent and pocketed it before sending the rest on to me, he announced that we had finally got down to real business with the Martini Fund. This fund I kept fairly fat, since it was an unwritten rule that for anything under $50.00, the regular agent's fee would automatically go into the fund. Of course, I soon caught on that I too was contributing 10 percent. The Martini Fund grew for the first few years, and we kept up its somewhat flexible level even when we both knew that we'd long since exhausted it on my annual trips to New York.

We drank amiably over many more years, with Henry averaging six Old Grandads to my one New York–style martini, either in his Fifth Avenue apartment or in his chosen somewhat-grubby watering holes, most of them reformed speakeasies, where I assumed that he was pretending vaguely that I was one of the girls of that period, rather than a middle-aged to elderly matron. He always stayed gentlemanly and apparently sober, although I cannot believe that he was anything but a good stiff drunk for the last forty-odd years of his life.

Henry's wife Natalie was a once-pretty woman indeed. I don't remember that she ever drank or smoked or did much but refuse categorically to travel in airplanes, or even automobiles at more than about thirty miles an hour. This restricted their wanderings, of course, and once in New York I could not but wince when she nerved herself to take a cab with me, and about ten feet from her door she started talking to the driver in a completely artificial five-year-old whine: "Mr. Driver-man, now don't you go too fast for little me," etc., etc. I almost threw up with embarrassment, and I understood something of Henry's constant leaning on his Old Grandad. As a matter of fact, though, I felt sorry for him and Natalie equally. And aside from his obvious attraction as one of the wittiest and most erudite men I ever met, I did not *like* either one of them very much. I was saddened by her death, which was quick and hard, of lung cancer from Henry's constant smoking of Gauloises Bleues. He felt a horrible guilt about this, and died in the same way but much slower and more painfully, less than a year after she had literally been killed by him. (And it was not coincidental that less than a year later his partner died too, of lung cancer caused by those same damned cigarettes. The tiny offices literally stank of their ineffable blue smoke.)

After Natalie's death and before Henry himself died, he got rather passionate about a woman somewhere in the South. I urged him to pursue this, the last time we met in New York, but he knew he was dying and did not want to entangle her. *Toujours le gentleman!* He surprised me that time by asking if he might kiss me, and I remember that we walked stiffly down into the gardens of his apartment house. He put his arms around me and gave me one long kiss right on the mouth, and his lips were very hot and dry and unpleasant, and of course I did not want to let him know how repelled I was by the thought of the cancer and so on that he stank of, especially since I was sure that he already knew it. That day, after the kiss, we walked without talking to a cab, and held hands feverishly for about half a minute, and then he directed the driver to take us to one of his favorite old pubs, and we killed any possible infection in a flood of booze. We talked a little bit about Natalie and his current southern love, and about who would succeed him as my literary agent, and I never saw him again. By now I don't remember his dried feverish hands and lips at all. They had nothing to do with the gentleman I knew and loved (and still do), and I'll never drink another martini without thinking of the fund. It still stands at the magic sum of $37.50, Henry's first and final proof that I would *never* be a best-seller.

—*Glen Ellen, California, 1988*

58

Ho-Hum Stuff

And now I'm trying to say something very clearly that I do not wish to say at all. As I talk, I feel wrong. This feeling is quite familiar to me, by now, and at times I do not think that it is worth putting down, but I shall *anyway!*

The true fact is that I think I may be starving to death. I really don't wish to, and I hope that nobody else wants it either, but one truth is that I am not hungry, and two others are that I really do not want to eat much and that I really don't care.

This is not at all what I meant to say, but I feel that there is a plot and, what is worse, I know this is silly and so am I. The whole idea is foolish and trite, but it is happening. It also concerns fears in other people of such things as alcoholism. Alcoholism I have never feared. I love to drink, but I've gone for months and years without doing so *because* I've not liked the people I had to drink with. For instance, when I was working in Hollywood, I almost never touched anything alcoholic, because I always went to cocktail parties and *appeared*—and Mike Romanoff's men protected me. One of them, a fat man I called Bacchus, would say very quietly to me, "Are you drinking white tonight?" And when I would say or nod a yes, he and his henchmen would serve me throughout the evening tall, stemmed, beautifully iced martini glasses filled with water, always with an olive or a little piece of lemon on a stick.

But now I seem to be cast in the role of a Heavy Drinker, although I've not touched anything alcoholic for more than forty-eight hours at least. I do keep the "three-bottle array" of gin, Campari, and vermouth on my little bureau in the passageway to the bathroom, and that same array is in the kitchen. It is used, and the replacements are noisily and often made, and nobody ever sees what I pour down the sink.

Today at noon while I lay on the bed listening to a new tape of John Updike stories, a mug of the mixture that is called *"my one-two-three"* was put down by my feet at the end of the bed, with a plate of nibbles. I had asked for these. They were made up· of a dab of chopped liver paste, which I made several days ago using Doro's recipe, and some cream cheese, and some spinach paste that I had invented and am rather proud of (reduce in olive oil one package of spinach, one chopped onion, and three cloves of garlic; put on stove to simmer until it is a paste), and some crackers or something crisp and fairly good. These and the almost ritualistic one-two-three were on a little table at the foot of the bed.

I was lying there, waiting for Marsha and unable to move, really, listening to John Updike and wondering again *why* Judith insists upon having him read his own stuff, and I gave a little kick to the table and it went clear across the room, and the mug of one-two-three broke, and the plate broke, and in general it was a mess. I was horrified.

Everything was made right, of course, but I was made to feel like an old drunk, and now there is another little plate of the remains on the same little table (now at the side of my bed instead of at the foot), and I have a cup of water there with a straw in it, and Marsha sits on the other side.

And for some reason the whole focus of this piece has changed as we sit together. And what I started to say about John Updike, and then about being hungry, or thinking I should be hungry, has shifted again. I honestly do think that very slowly and surely and neatly I am being put away, changed into a kind of clumsy oaf with no real thought or sensitivity.

I know full well that this is a common fallacy of elderly or aging people. I am one of these, of course, and I am astonished to find myself actually believing such nonsense. I *don't* believe it, and yet I do. I've written a lot about aging for fifty years myself, and I've read most of the plays and stories and so on about it, in both English and American, and I have smiled and suffered through them too. It seems important that I'm now thinking this—and I still do think I'm partly right!

There was a pause here, a kind of regrouping of thoughts. Marsha went down (or did not go down?) to the highway for the mail. I called David to tell him so. Or did he already know? Barbara came in or went out; she was peevish about something or other, possibly because she thought she had delivered the mail, yet Marsha had gone down for it, and so on. She may or may not be back tonight for supper. She said as she went out that I could have some chopped liver, cream cheese, spinach paste, if I wished.

I do not think I wish to, because I just ate a mouthful of the stuff on the second plate that was left here, and had crunched my way doggedly through a shard of pottery or glass from the remains of the first batch that had been scraped up some time ago, after I kicked it heedlessly across the floor.

So I think that I am probably still hungry. I do not feel so. I may or may not eat more, but at this minute I'm rolling between my fingers a piece of green pottery from that first inadvertent tossing of the stuff across the room.

All this seems really ridiculous as I say it, but I would and do agree with many of my mentors that it may clear some inner airs— not to mention graces!—to speak of it. (This business of spitting out pieces of china bores me.) Now I must think of what to do. Instinctively, I think I should let things slide on, and not protest in any way the inevitable reliving of an old old story. In my case, as in countless others that I know about, it is almost too banal to bother with, and I would really rather not. However . . . (And here I don't know quite how to finish. But I do not like this whole business. It seems clear to me in my head, yet by the time I ask Marsha to copy it down as I say it, it sounds almost too dull to put on paper. I'll try to sum it up now, and then Marsha and I will dictate some beautiful fan mail.) However, I do honestly believe that I am the victim of my own body, as well as of the designs of several others. I am being starved . . . and this is partly because I am not interested in the food. Yet I *can* eat, so that I can blame possible starvation on other people rather than on my own intellectual and physical deeds.

I do not look forward to supper. I'm going to make another railroad sandwich of local disrepute and renown (and by local, I mean familial, because my family has always been highly amused by them), but when Barbara said she was going away for the night again and I told her that I wished she would stay because I wanted and needed her to be here, she said in a laughing way that is peculiarly hers that she could not stomach the thought of another railroad sandwich, and that she hoped she would never see or hear of one ever again. I said that people were amused by them, and she said that she was not, and then she left. Then Marsha came back from doing the silly errand for David (and here I do not really mean silly!), and I pulled that piece of green porcelain out from between two teeth, and now we're going to work.

I hope that this will be some indication of my puzzlements. I honestly feel that I am dying of starvation, perhaps helped unwittingly by outside forces. On the other hand, I'm actually glad to do this (do I mean *die now?*), and I do not wish to implicate any human being in any way at all. If someone does want me to die, I do not feel that there is a reason for it except that I may be taking up necessary breathing space on the planet. (Perhaps I do not like to be reminded of this?) There cannot be any pecuniary interest here, as there was in some of the old stories I used to know about elderly duchesses and so on who were artfully done in by their butlers. So if there is indeed any malice in this plot, it is probably based on physical envy: I am taller, or older, or better known socially or in a worldly way—things like that. Yes, if it indeed exists, it is probably based on some kind of envy.

I recognize this and I feel very sad about it, and I think that is my story for now.

—Glen Ellen, California, 1988

 59

Anon.

I know, I *feel,* something about the anonymity of being a bag lady. I want it. But my training is against this escape from responsibility, the escape into what this lack of responsibility might mean. I don't want to run away, to shuck off the natural "burdens." But I want to be *anonymous.* And how can one ever be, except by escaping, running away, hiding? No, I'll probably stay . . .

—Glen Ellen, California, 1989

60

My Grown-Up Ears

One of the best parts about growing older for me is that I am increasingly able to watch myself do so.

Even a few years ago, a new step toward my maturity would happen without any obvious warning, so that I'd find myself, some soft gray day, doing or thinking or speaking in a way that would have been impossible the sunny day before. But now, I am more conscious of my own peculiar speeds.

I know that I am fairly slow. I acknowledge, without too much impatience, that it may take me several years to reach this or that stage of adult behavior, in spite of graying hairs and such, and I feel a kind of smug relief that I have developed so neatly, if at all, this far.

I was sure for at least ten years before it finally happened that someday I would be able to hear chamber music for more than half an hour at a time without strain. I knew too that there was no use worrying about my backwardness; it would change gradually and surely. And it did, so that at this point the intricate orderly notes of four stringed instruments playing together are almost the only kind I can actually listen to, and I am exasperated by classical "symphonies," which even a few months ago touched the quick. I admit without perturbation the possibility that if I live long enough, my spiritual ear may reshape itself to such a point that it will tolerate only the sound of a flute, or a Chinese whistle tied to a pigeon's wing.

It was much the same about reading the Bible. For a long time it did not matter whether I would ever like it, and then when I matured enough to know that it would eventually be important to me, I was able to wait patiently. I had no idea of when it would happen, just as I had had none about the place and time that would suddenly find me listening with my inside ears, my grown-up ears, to a Beethoven quartet. That is why I am thankful that the time did come: it is over with, so that I need no longer wait.

It was in August 1945, and I was sitting in the North Reading Room of the New York Public Library. There was heavy dark rain falling, and the enormous hall was full of the scratchy rustlings and the smell of unaired clothes inevitable when many research workers congregate. I was grubbing in a concordance, looking up some such word as *gluttony* and thumbing here and there in a very neat practical copy of the King James Version.

And then I was reading:

"In the beginning . . . "

The words came out clear and strong and in a most beautiful order. They were the most straightforward words I had ever read, and although they were familiar to me from my youngest day, I knew that I had never really heard them before. I read for many hours without any knowledge of time or weariness, and when I finally went out into the wet street, I felt a sense of great relief that the time had come, that the waiting was over, that I had grown up that much more. It was probably a little the way a woman who has long wanted a child feels when she knows that at last she has conceived. The thing had finally happened, and it was rich with promise.

My mother's mother, when I was a little child, lived with us. She was what was known then as "religious." There were many like her, strange products of the Victorian era: women who remained unsatisfied by constant childbearing and the portly bearded courtesies extended to them by their husbands, and who fed all their secret hungers through a fanatical and at times almost orgiastic devotion to one of the many austere Protestant sects that flourished for them and because of them.

Grandmother was a Campbellite or, as she preferred to call herself and her fellow church members, a "Christian." She was of course the dominating figure in her church, as everywhere, and as she grew older she increased her importance by giving almost all of her money to the various ministers, organ funds, and missionaries (all starving, vicariously or in actuality) that touched her golden circle. People bowed to her, and flattered her, and cadged shamelessly from her in spite of their real respect, and she flourished, and was happier than she had ever been in the ample bosom of her philoprogenitive family.

It is probably fortunate that she died before my generation reached an articulate state, but between my third and sixth year, she did what she could to prepare me to be a "Christian."

I went to Sunday school and church every week with her, and enjoyed it very much. Everybody paid the two of us extravagant compliments: "What a lovely picture they make—old lady, with her sweet little granddaughter, and perhaps today is the day to mention the ministerial pension fund again to that wonderful old dowager . . ." And even Grandmother was not optimistic enough to trust my interest in God's word, thundered or squeaked from the pulpit, without bolstering it with an occasional snippet of butterscotch or barley sugar slipped to me from her crocheted handbag.

After Sunday dinner, which consisted mainly of bland pale boiled things like old hens and dumplings, and flaccid puddings because of Grandmother's Nervous Stomach (a condition that almost always accompanied the more virtuous attributes of such female Victorian churchgoers, for reasons obvious to any amateur Freudian), she napped and I raced through the funny papers with my little sister—*The Katzenjammer Kids* and *Mutt and Jeff.* By the time she awoke and straightened the intricate cheaters that lay within her famous silver pompadour, we were lying decorously on the floor, deep in one of the many books about Christianity that she bought from deserving young divinity students and gave to us every Christmas and birthday.

Our interest was genuine: they were ingenious books, at least, and we liked the games they made of knowing the names of the Twelve Apostles and such. There was one, our favorite, that told most of the Old Testament stories in a kind of sign language: God was a mysterious symbol, perhaps the Jewish capital letter for Jehovah with a little piece of fire around it, and Adam was a little man behind a very large fig leaf, and all the birds and beasts of the story of creation were reasonable facsimiles of themselves, strung together with a few monosyllables to make the Holy Bible "fun for tiny tots."

Perhaps that is a good idea, but I do not think so. It was, as I reflect upon it, a complete vulgarization, done without sensibility, presented in a crude manner that could appeal only fleetingly even to five-year-old minds. It partially succeeded in reducing the Scriptures to the level of *Mutt and Jeff* and *The Katzenjammer Kids,* but I do not think it did anything at all to interest us in either the temporal or spiritual meanings of the stories it told. We might better, to my mind, have been reading or listening to less significant tales.

Sunday school did nothing but bore me. It turned all the excitement and clash and turmoil of the Old Testament to dust, and reduced the mystery of Jesus' life and death to a self-consciously painful confusion. After my confirmation, which seemed to reassure my parents about something or other but crystallized my own feelings into a quiet but firm rebellion, I became an agnostic.

When I went away to a church preparatory school, I got high grades for several years in the required Bible course, and knew Hebrew dates backwards and forwards, and five minutes after summer vacation started could not remember one word of what I had learned.

It was the same in college, except that there I was trying to convince myself, with the other self-styled intellectuals, that the Bible, "if considered solely as a fascinating collection of myths and legends" and so on and so on, was Great Literature. I was stirred as any young human must be by the passion and sensuality of some of the songs I read in it, and I admitted glibly that it would be wonderful to be able to "believe" in it.

Almost before I had finished talking that way, I began to laugh at other people who did, and for several years dismissed the whole thing from my life, except for a feeling of scornful impatience now and then when I heard of older people who read the Bible from cover to cover once a year, or did some other such narcotic trick.

Once, many years ago, I tried to read it in a time of deep sadness, but it was dead to me. I would have been grateful for any comfort then, and I wondered why I could find none in what had plainly stayed many another like me.

Then, as I began to recognize the pace of my gradual development, and saw myself waiting patiently for the moments when I would really taste lentil soup or hear every note in a trio or know what the bird said in a Chinese wall painting, I realized that at some time I would be able to read the Bible. And now I am.

It is not the fault of my grandmother or boredom or my own stupidity that it took so long. I was simply incapable of it, until the summer of 1945. Since then, oh rich fortunate me, I can go almost anywhere in it. The violence and the plottings and the blood and tenderness are more exciting than in any book I have ever read, I think, and they are told in a better simpler style. And the mystery of man and his faith, if no clearer to me, shows itself like a thread of water, forever flowing round and round the world.

For when Israel sang a little song to the well—"Spring up, O well; sing ye unto it"—and the well did spring up to slake his people's thirst, and when I remember that wandering Arabian tribes still sing thus to their wells, I know more about faith than I ever thought I would, and I am glad of it.

—*Glen Ellen, California, 1989*

61

The Best Meal
I Ever Ate

One of the most universal questions and therefore the one left most unanswered is "What is the best meal you ever ate?" It is almost impossible to answer, honestly anyway, so I can only reply that I don't know! I am as incapable of deciding this as I am of saying that such-and-such is the best novel I ever read, or so-and-so is the best painting I ever saw.

What I can do, however, and with very little hesitation, is to name the *most important* meal I ever ate, the one that for both known and unknown reasons came to have the greatest significance in the pattern of my life. (The gastronomical quality of the food in that meal, of course, had very little to do with its importance.)

I can say almost to the minute when I ate it, and although I cannot recall exactly what it was made up of, I must confess that it was a comparatively mediocre noonday dinner, as such feasts go on the overcrowded stuffy boat trains running between Cherbourg and Paris.

I remember that the train was wide open to the hot September air, so that cinders swirled everywhere in the cluttered second-class compartments. People pushed—harried traveling men, timid students and tourists, overworked waiters winging deftly along the aisles with their great trays of steaming scalloped veal and white beans and suchlike.

But I was eating the most important meal of my life, I believe. In truth I was absorbing it through every pore of my spiritual skin. I was breathing it, cinders and all, into the depths of my heart. As I looked out over the stained cloth, past the half-empty wine bottles and the flushed concentration of the strangers I dined with, I knew that I was, from that moment on, a thinking human being instead of a healthy young animal.

Everything that had happened in my life seemed, there in the rackety train with the tiny green meadows wheeling past me and the little sleek brown cows and the apple trees, part of the preparation for this Right Moment. I felt, and possibly it was so, that I had never been as conscious. Suddenly I recognized my own possibilities as a *person,* and I was almost stunned by the knowledge that never again would I eat or drink as I had done for my first twenty years, sanely and well but unthinkingly.

The first taste of bread, that day: it came in chunks, chopped from loaves four feet long stacked at the end of the dining car like skis, and it was the best bread I had ever eaten and I knew that forever, as of that noontime, I would be intolerant of the packaged puffy stuff called bread at home.

The salad, mixed roughly in a great bowl and shoved from one untidy table to the next along the car: it was made of very ordinary oil and vinegar, cinders and a few small bugs and beetles, and piles of the most wonderful garden lettuces I had ever tasted, long, short, dark green and light, bitter in this leaf and almost sweet in that. Never again, I knew fatalistically, would I more than tolerate the neat, bug-free, and almost completely tasteless salad stuff sold in stores at home.

And the little rolls of cream cheese called *petits-suisses,* and the trays of tiny gnarled apples, and the bitter coffee, and the crude good wine poured from a common bottle on each table: it sounds almost disrespectful to say it, but even the astonishing events of the past several weeks or so seemed but a logical preparation for this moment! Falling in love for the first time since I was nine, being married for the first time at all, crossing the Atlantic for the first time ("student third," but on the *Berengaria!*)—they all led irrevocably to 1:43 P.M., September 25, 1929, when I picked up a last delicious crust crumb from the table, smiled dazedly at my love, peered incredulously at a great cathedral on the horizon, and recognized myself as a newborn sentient human being, ready at last to *live.*

Healthy digestion took command of me, both physically and in my soul, for I had just eaten, not the best meal of my life, but the most important one—and at the Right Moment.

—Glen Ellen, California, 1989

62

Reading Aloud

I am fortunate indeed that everyone I know likes to read aloud. They usually do it quite well too, and I do not mention that I could do much better myself, since I have been reading aloud since I was about five years old. I started then with the only thing I knew, which was the Old Testament of the King James Version, as I read it syllable by syllable in my highest voice to my Grandmother Holbrook. I would go from her knees, where I leaned my head while I sat on a very little stool at her feet, directly to the cook's toilet on the back porch where I would crouch at the feet of my little sister Anne. And I would read in the same high voice to her what I had just learned from Grandmother, while Anne did her job on the toilet.

This was a lengthy process, and it was easy for me to repeat several earlier lessons, for our mutual enjoyment, before her job was done. I went from the Old Testament directly to the *Five Little Peppers* series, every volume from the first clear through to the end, or at least until the older Pepper boy got to the kissing age. Anne and I thought this was very silly, and I always stopped at the first kiss. Fortunately the children's series were almost endless, and in some few there was no kissing at all. *The Motor Girls* was one, and as I remember there was no kissing at all in *The Motor Boys* nor in any of the continued stories in *The Youth's Companion, Chatter Box,* and *John Martin's Magazine for Children.* These three weeklies, or perhaps monthlies, were more trustworthy than almost any serials, and they did much for good daily habits and evacuation as well.

The *Little Colonel* series was honest and decent and upstanding and all that Christian rubbish until the last volume, as I remember. It was called *The Little Colonel's Knight Comes Riding,* and we knew from the very beginning that we would never finish it. I read bravely through the first flutterings of her girlish heart, but soon after the third chapter Anne began to make disgusting noises above my head, and I tried to titter, but soon felt like throwing up, and that was the end of the Little Colonel for us both forever. (Much later I heard that the Little Colonel was very racist, but the black-white angle was completely ignored by us there on the porch toilet; it was love love love that induced our puking rejections.) .

We read several more series of nonromantic quasi fiction, both in the toilet and up in our own bedroom where we hid in the closet and read by the thin light of one bulb high in the ceiling, which I pulled on and off by a long piece of string, so that I must have been at least eight by then. Of course we could have read in bed, at least until the lights were turned out at the door by my mother at 7:30, but we were used to enjoying fiction in a crouching position, and for two or three more years the dimly lit and probably rather smelly little closet was our chosen spot for the hidden pleasure of my reading aloud and Anne's listening. I wonder now if that explains any of my well-hidden aversion to being read to by anyone. Somehow I cannot quite imagine pretending to be my little sister sitting on a toilet, listening avidly to my dignified friends reading to me in a crouching position at my feet.

I think we hit bottom, if I may say so, in this latrine routine with *The Water-Babies,* written by Charles Kingsley. Here I am haunted still by that atmosphere so that I titter and think of water closets and privies and such things when I mention that small classic, and I can't remember just how or why the hero grows up enough to kiss a girl. We stopped abruptly and went into almost-preadolescent titters, loud noises of assumed pure disgust, because suddenly we realized that we too were interested in his wanting to kiss somebody. Our innocence was gone, and as a matter of fact, I don't think I read aloud again to my sister Anne, and neither one of us ever finished *The Water-Babies,* even silently. So to this day some seventy years later, I don't know how it ends, and Anne surely did not bother to find out before she died when she was fifty-five a long time ago.

By now I guard my ability to read almost ferociously. I know that I can read anything in this world if I must, and I may have to someday. Meanwhile I do not even read the address on envelopes; I hand them to L. or to Marsha to open and read them to me. L. read a short thing to me recently, and we have devised a cruelly efficient way of disposing of other people's manuscripts. It consists of three moves, and I think is fair enough, although perhaps it is silly of me to boast of it, in case . . . so I'll stop. But I can state honestly that it is fair and entails some real work on the part of both the reader and me.

Reading in itself is such a privilege, even secondhand, that it seems impossible to think of it in such terms as mine. It is true, however, that my sister and I learned from the Old Testament more than we could ever know any other way about the beauty of the language. By now I thank God that it was the King James

Version that we learned from. It is almost purification of the body as well as of the soul, and I can claim this now, in a room with black tile floors with fresh air coming in the window, just as clearly as I could in the toilet on the back porch, or upstairs in our equally smelly little closet.

There was something wonderful about the privacy of those first readings, and perhaps this explains why I do not like to go to public readings by a famous actor or writer.

There is also something about being read to that is completely different from reading. But both are honorable pursuits and greatly to be desired. When I was taught to read by my Grandmother Holbrook, I read in a loud, rather piping voice and without any expression at all, but correctly, straight through the Old Testament. I can remember the click of my grandmother's knitting needles above my head and how I became aware gradually that I was outgrowing the little stool on which I sat. I had settled down on her feet before we finished the Old Testament and I graduated to the New Testament—much less interesting and never to be finished, at least not while my head was against those knees.

I have always known that I was fortunate indeed to have a grandmother who insisted that the King James Version was the most wonderful way in the world to learn the value and beauty of the printed word.

A long time after these first lessons, but still years ago by now, I understood completely why Joseph Conrad's prose is as clear and simple as it is: he said that when he was a Polish sailor and stood watch at night, he would read one page from his pocket version of the King James Bible and tear it out and light his pipe with it and think about what he had read for the rest of the night. Of course I was never a Polish sailor, but I do feel that King James's language helped me learn to speak English with some of the same respect and simplicity that Conrad put into his writing.

I no longer use a crouching position when I read aloud, now that I have grown up a little more. But these early experiences may explain why I prefer to read to myself rather than be read to, even by another trusted and loved person. And the idea of going to a theater and being part of an audience and listening to a single voice reading something classical from the stage is almost nauseating to me.

My own voice is no longer piping and young, but it has been used often and well to read to people who loved me: my sister Anne and later my first husband Al Fisher, to whom I read everything ever translated from Russian into English by Constance Garnett. I think I read *War and Peace* twice or three times aloud. This seems impossible now, when I can't stand the thought of reading it even to myself.

—*Glen Ellen, California, 1989*

63

Frustration—II
(Final Scream)

6,9.23456789 89—which is to say, December 6, 1989 . . . And there is little point in my trying to type further. The performance will not be a good one.

I feel that I must try somehow to make a real change, though I am in a very angry mood, which I . . . This is an almost violent change, from the occasional frustration that has been eating into my bones for too long now.

Perhaps it has peaked. Or perhaps it is very bad, and is already a very present evil, a true danger to my reason.

The anger is a relief. I hope that I can hold on to it long enough to recognize it. I need it as a kind of ally.

The frustration is poisonous. I recognize its real strength and I fear it. Of course, I know the evil of anger too. But it makes a welcome change.

This may not really be legible. That is a chance I must take. Marsha must just try to figure out this typing.

My state of dangerous frustration is justified. And I think that the gradual changeover to real anger will be healthy. I pray so. I am angry because I think it is unfair that at this stage of my life when I should be in real control of the natural talent I have been developing for so many years, which is probably at its peak—yes, it seems unfair that I now find myself too blind to read, or even to type, and I cannot write legibly. And by now my voice has grown too uncertain to be used for dictating.

Here I was interrupted, so I cannot remember how many things I listed to make for such a long messy collection of frustrations. I know that I did name my increasing loss of sight. This is very bad, and I feel that there is little hope of any improvement. Sometimes I feel that I should make some pact, in any form—sell my soul— to give me the feeling for even a few hours, of being able to work once more with my own eyes, on notes that I know are everywhere waiting for my eyes alone—notes I have waiting in boxes at the end of the room.

7. xii. 89

What I typed last night may well be useless. This new attempt will perhaps be equally so—before it is stopped by Nina, who tries to protect me against my selfish wishes. She made me stop typing last night, so tonight I have started before Marsha leaves. I am sure that very soon now Nina will come in and try to convince me that I am too tired to work. But I am determined to go on until 6:00 P.M., when I am supposed to eat supper while I watch *Cheers* on TV. Perhaps I will at least have time to report that I am still very angry. I hope that something good will come of it. The mountain of frustration, which I *surely* mentioned last night, has changed in the past twenty-four hours into plain anger, which I'm surprised to find almost enjoyable. I am not yet sure why; basically I despise anger as such. I think it is a destructive and dangerous and poisonous emotion especially when it appears to be so welcome. I pray that it will soon change into something positive.

Productive is the word.

I must escape from this present *meaningless* state. It is essential, and it is just as well that I cannot understand why I am speaking now with heartily emphasized words: ESSENTIAL. ANGER. DANGER. PRODUCE. CHANGE.

Of course I shall always think it very unfair that I of all people should find myself unable to read or write or even speak—speak even clearly enough to use cassettes during the evening hours when I feel very alert, almost all of every night. But I refuse to stop. This sounds like pathetic bravado at best. I know it may well be all of that. But I do feel that an answer to some of the physical problems will evolve. It must. It has to and it will, and meanwhile I will try to do something more coherent, and soon, about putting some order into my papers. This may mean some sort of showdown, or even some kind of break with L. P. and even with N. K. B. I pray not, in either case, but of course mostly with Norah. No, that will not come about. Impossible.

A break with L. P. is more possible, although I don't want that either. At present, she does me no real good, but that too will change, if I can maintain my present air of subtle independence from her, and hide my real exasperation at her clumsy confusing chaotic attempts to put the many boxes of papers that she seems to have accumulated at the end of this room into some semblance of order. She comes two mornings a week, and if I am actively unpleasant with her, as I have been for the last two times, she will work for about an hour each day. I suspect that she *feels* that she works much longer and harder than that. I am also sure that she expects me to pay her according to her own scale. This I shall, but not until after the new year.

L. P. has no idea of sustained work. I taught her nothing, much as I wanted to, while we played with the book. I was a real failure there—except that I brought off a really dirty bit of play, and without any denying from her, I got her to sign what she herself called a book. When we started work, I soon realized that she had no qualms at all about changing any of my own prose as she transcribed the tapes. Initially, this annoyed me, mainly because my way of saying things was demonstrably different from hers. But when I realized that she did not see the differences at all, and felt that she was actually improving what I had added, I gave up. Before the end of our work, she was perhaps a little sheepish about this, and sent her final transcription off unread by me to her agent.

Ho hum. But I thought no real harm had been done to either of us. I encourage her almost daily to write, to finish some of the four or five things she has started since she first came into my picture. I continue to feel that she has enormous potential and, above all, creative energy. But it must be directed by someone stronger and more disciplined than she, and I am not strong enough. Nor am I willing to develop and in other ways carry her, especially now when I find myself almost powerless to do anything for my own self. Fortunately I don't think L. P. will ever find this out. Nor will she know that I really despair and feel somewhat ashamed of myself that I cannot do more.

It is the next day. I am appalled, in a mild way that is very offensive really, to realize that my anger, which I welcomed as a change from my frantic sense of frustration, may well become a kind of apathetic near peace. By now I don't even feel anger, the painful absorbing kind. I feel apathetic.

One proof of this latest change is that since the morning, only four hours ago, I think, I realize that I am no longer snarling and biting at myself as any frustrated animal does. I have escaped the trap, which is what I was trying to do, of course. I knew immediately that the frustration had changed during the night, because for the first time in longer than I can remember I slept for almost eight hours, and I shifted at least once during the night without any real planning. This planning has been necessary for a long time. Moving is often very painful, and every shift of my body is carefully rehearsed before I move one knee, for instance.

Well, it was 4:00 in the morning when I realized that I had slept without even thinking of shifting my body, and I knew that great changes had either happened or would soon come about.

And when I saw that I was no longer a helpless mess, a subhuman sick thing, but that I was instead an angry woman, that I was in a contained and tightly controlled rage, then I felt released, actually happy. It meant that I was still capable of change. But always there was the lurking sense of resignation. When I wrote Georges Connes that I felt quite philosophical about living at the Ranch with Father and raising the two children after I got the divorce from Donald Friede, Georges wrote back something like "You are not feeling philosophical, you are simply resigned."

And he was right, of course.

But this time I hope that this present almost cozy state, this comfortable condition, complete with several hours of untroubled sleep, does not mean that I have indeed GIVEN UP.

I honestly do not want to be comfortable and free from the mental frettings and much of the actual pain and discomfort that have for some time kept me as I still am—an aged female, almost bedridden, fighting an almost devastating weariness. There are times when I must steel myself to get to my feet, or even move one hand a few inches—

And here I could scream in silent impotent rage at the cruel fact that I cannot read what I have just written, so that I cannot in turn even finish this sentence. That is *very disquieting,* to put it mildly. I hate long involuted sentences. I realize that several times in these last few days of trying to write, I have gotten completely out of hand. It is worth apologizing to Marsha and Pat, if I decide to let them see this final scream or whatever it might be called. If it makes any sense at all, it may serve as a summing up of my long life of writing. I don't know now if anyone will bother to look at my journals, but when I could still see enough to look at two or three of them I was struck by my preoccupation with writing.

It is true that I always knew that I could write better than most people, but it is also true that I never thought myself of any importance at all in this field. That is why I always denied the often mocking remark that anyone who keeps a journal does so only to have it read. I did keep a journal but I never thought it would be read. I can't remember now, but perhaps I have left notes about my ideas about writing that may be of some value, after I have died, to people who are interested in the very slow process, if any, of me, M.F.K.F., mainly because I am not a writer at all. I was born with a somewhat keener way of using words than average people have. I also enjoy using words simply and honestly.

But the present flurry of interest in Fisher is not because I write better than most, but simply because I write now much as I did more than fifty years ago. In other words, I have stayed simple, and I am basically a simple person.

And right now I regret, more than I can say, that I must stop writing this. I am physically very tired. It is time to call for some lunch to be brought to me. I'll eat it on my bed, and wait for

Norah to come for the night. I hope I will have some voice for her; I want very much to work with her. I must get the work on the Dijon book under way. This is an urgent matter, more urgent than any other.

Of course, she could do it alone, perhaps having to carry on if I should die before it is done.

—Glen Ellen, California, 1989

64
Style

Now and then critics have referred to my writing "style," or called me a "stylist." This always astonishes me, and makes me feel embarrassed.

I have thought of people like Henry James as a "stylist," in our Anglo-American language, and perhaps somebody like George Santayana, but the so-called style of such writers bores me, turns me off, makes me feel tricked. Joseph Conrad was more frankly a seeker of a "manner of writing," as the *Oxford English Dictionary* calls style, but it does not matter if he ever occupied himself with it. Vladimir Nabokov, another example of this preoccupation with the rhythmic use of words, shines with the same strange luster of an acquired tongue, always shaping phrases and using them through and back to his native sounds—Poland, Russia.

Perhaps this happens in all of us, if we have the right chemistry. I was never born to be a real stylist, because I am limited compared to anyone I may mention in the writing game. But how can I know how far back I may have gone in the womb, listening to the way words can be used?

Meanwhile it continues to amaze me that anyone might think that what I have written has "style." I have never thought about this until lately, when the word has come up.

It has always seemed to me that the American language, which is what I have spoken from birth, is perhaps more alive and better suited than any other in the world to life as we live it. The French way of speaking pleases me, and I have been greatly helped in the use of my own tongue by my petty but intense study of the grammar and syntax I learned in Dijon long ago. By now my accent and my control are faltering, but I still dream and converse silently in fairly passable French, and what I have learned from it has made my use of American much clearer and firmer.

When I was about twelve, my father wanted all of his children to learn Spanish, and he was right: we should have, because we lived in the recently Americanized country of southern California. The man who came to teach us was Señor Cobos, the Quaker minister out in Jimtown, and a protégé of my father, but it was impossible to learn correct grammar from him when I already knew gutter Mex from my best friends in school. Later I studied proper Spanish in high school and breezed through it without any real interest.

Latin was different. I flunked the first year. My teacher burst into violent tears, and was sent off to a mountain rest home for two weeks, when I did my first essay on Caesar's cold-blooded invasions of Gaul. It was all in Latin, or so I thought. I tried again, the next semester, and passed, without the slightest idea that I was learning a lot that I still know about my own use of words and sentences and phrases. (My teacher felt all right the second time— resigned, anyway.)

I now wish that children could be taught basic grammar, in

Latin preferably, when they start in the first grade. Except for my one searing humiliation with Caesar, I never learned any grammar at all when I was going to school. This was because I came from an articulate family that did not split infinitives and so on, so that it was assumed that I knew a noun from an adjective.

I did not, until I went to France. It was there that I learned humility as well as what could be done with nouns and adjectives and their capacity for the finest honing. For the first time in my life I worked and I understood. It was like electricity. Nothing was easy. There, nobody cared if my father was the editor of the newspaper and my mother had studied in Dresden, and I was pitcher on the girls' baseball team and teacher's pet.

—Glen Ellen, California, 1989

65

Zapping

Unsent letter

Dear K.:

Today is a wonderful day, really the first one of spring for me for some reason. I feel like dancing, whirling around any old way. It is astonishing and above all frightening, though, to realize that even before I am thinking this, I know that it is not possible. I couldn't dance if I had to. Actually I feel stiff and full of aches and pains, and why not? I am past eighty years old, and more than full of the usual woes—but I look out the window and it's so damned beautiful that really I am dancing. In other words, I feel quite silly today. What is even worse is that I would be willing to bet you ten cents or ten thousand cold ducats or whatever that you'd dance too. We'd go whirling off together.

Of course I got your letter, and you do indeed sound woeful. In fact, the letter is so damned miserable that it is very funny to me, and I don't mind telling you so right now along with all this dancing, which I am really doing. I am also laughing very hard. And all this goes on invisibly and inaudibly.

Of course, dear K., I've had a cataract operation. It was quite a while ago, and it went off very well indeed. I never felt as if I had two eyes in one socket, though. I am sorry you do, although really wouldn't two eyes be better than one, especially if they both work? As for the laser operation, I doubt that you will feel anything, except of course the boredom of having to go to the doctor's office and sit still for even a second or two.

Does your doctor say "zap"? The last time I saw mine, in Santa Rosa, he told me that of course he could zap me whenever I said to, but that he saw no point at all in zapping anybody who was as unzappable as I. Why bother? he asked. Quite possibly he would have to do it over and over. Why spend the money on it? I can make it with the help of other people, he said in a companionable, warm affectionate way. So I agreed, feeling properly warm and affectionate myself. But it's nice to know that I can be zapped whenever I feel like it *and* that he would do it. And I really do like him for talking to me that way. Maybe you have his twin zapping away at you.

I do agree with you that "something peculiar happens every minute" to make old age so "fascinating." Fascinating should be in quotes too because you said it when I would not. I do think, though, that aging is a very busy time. It can also be horribly expensive, "usually in a doctor's office," as you say. I am appalled to find or think of how much it costs to stay alive as one ages, and especially if kindly doctors are breathing down your neck every time some new symptom pops up. Symptom of what, though? I suppose deterioration implies that there is a constant process of disintegration or spoiling, but I don't see why these many aspects are called symptoms. The trouble with this steady fading away is that every aspect of it is viewed with alarm and is generally found unacceptable, when really it is the natural thing and is symptomatic of nothing at all. Doctors grow rich on it of course, and I often wonder why and how we are kept so ignorant of what is really a natural process. So one eye grows dimmer, and to protect its dimness a film forms over it. Help help help, and doctors are called in and operations are proposed and then performed as if each time it happened it was actually an unheard-of new development instead of something to be expected and prepared for.

So you had a cataract removed. It was the first time, plainly, and you wrote to me, "Ever had a cataract operation?" etc., etc., and I was amused and now I feel rather testy about it. "Of course," I said, and then I got even testier. The word *laser* made me angry too, after my first feeling of amusement and general danciness about it being spring today, with the new leaves looking very twinkly in the bright still pool of sunshine of midmorning. By now the words *cataract* and *laser* make me feel almost *angry*—not even testy but peevish, really peevish. Hell, I say, why does K. think he's the only man in the world who's ever had a bum eye? But is it really bum, or is it merely a signal that he is getting older, and does that mean that K., of all people, is caught in this silly syndrome of believing that he alone is fearing and hating aging? Hell and damnation, I say. This can't happen to K. Surely he more than most people has long since faced the fact that if he grows to be past fifty, chronologically anyway, he must perforce accept certain changes in his body. Yes, a little film will form over one eye, and then over the other perhaps, and he will feel astonished and finally he'll tell somebody about it. And then the doctors will move in, not because they are cruel or mean, but because they too must eat. And the jig's up. They will trot out little lasers that cost millions of dollars to operate, and they will make little tiny slits and marks on his most precious eyes, and he will shake and tremble and many people like me will laugh because they too shook and trembled. And we will all pay and pay, and the doctors finally will get little films over their eyes and they too will shake and tremble a little, and we all will be pouring out money and grumbling and fuming —and even dancing in the springtime.

In other words, K., I am as appalled as I always am at how completely unprepared we are for this inevitable game. What is most surprising probably is that I don't want anyone to be surprised (and by "anyone" here, I mean anyone that I love). I seem to think that if I love a person, he or she will perforce be above such common continuing universal things like fear and astonishment and anger and pain. I want people like you to know from the minute you are born that if you live long enough, you will of course find your eyes growing filmy, etc., etc. You will grow older. You will deteriorate. I do and you do, because we are both human beings and we are exactly like every other human being, except perhaps we are more fortunate because we admit it. And admitting that you are human makes it inevitable that you must admit to growing older, if indeed you are fortunate enough to grow old, and even to deteriorate, disintegrate, fall apart, and finally die. I am very fussy about words, as you know, and here I use the word *fortunate* with great care. I honestly do feel that anyone who can live decently, or even with some difficulty into and past middle age, and then attain old age is lucky. He is *fortunate*.

This does sound rather Pollyannaish, at least superficially. But it is a statement that I don't make lightly and, I am quite sure, not foolishly either. This is because I am old myself, and I know I have experienced many of the less pleasant aspects of deterioration. Actual years do not count, though. Often the symptoms that I am now feeling (and here I could say enduring or surviving or experiencing) have been felt by people much younger, men or women perhaps in their sixties or seventies. Of course I have heard of people almost 100 who swear they are not crickety and have all their own teeth, etc., etc. They are, to put it clinically or coldly, plain freaks. (Or liars!) You and I are absolutely normal just like countless millions of others in our same sorry, lamentable, miserable condition. So we sigh and moan, and call the doctor for some help, and everybody feels much better to have passed along his misery from himself to another human being.

And yet I am telling you how nice it is to feel dancy. Really, it is laughable, this part of the whole aging business, for me anyway. This constant contradiction in terms. I should be commiserating with you, which means with myself. Instead I am teasing you and therefore myself. Poor K.! You just had a cataract operation and on March 31 you are going to have a laser deal, and then you say, "Keep as well as may be" to me. And I can hear your sadness and your feeling of dismay and astonishment that this has happened to you. And all I can feel is real annoyance with you. *Of course* you are sad, miserable, and so on. And you know damned well that I am sad and miserable for you. But, and here I do mean a great big fat *BUT,* surely you must in some way have been prepared for this dreadful condition. You must have known somewhere along the line that you were bound to feel sadder and more miserable than you had in your whole life—you must have *known,* K., that if you lived past seventy you would ache and hurt and things would grow misty and so on and that you would endure them all.

I do think that women have it over men here. They are more accepting. And perhaps they are less hurt by actual pain and sorrow than are men. I do not mean that it is their lot to accept suffering and grief. I do think, though, that they make less fuss about some things, basic things, like hurting and dying and so on than men seem to do.

If this is the case, I am luckier than you. I am not sure, though. I know that I feel awful today, for instance, but that it would not occur to me to say so. I tell myself that I feel this way or that way, but I am very matter-of-fact about it. If I were a man, there would be more surprise and astonishment, as well as futile anger, in any such admission.

In your letter you betray, to me at least, your real fear and petulance and fury too. I am truly sorry about all this. I don't sound as if I am, but it is true, and the main trouble, I think, is that you were unprepared for what is happening to you. All your life you have seen other people spoil, deteriorate, fade away, and yet you have never really accepted the fact that it would happen to you too. I suppose this is the difference between empathy and sympathy. It would be very easy to remain pedantic and distant and keep it all a question of words, period, with or without any wisdom behind them. That, though, would be too easy. I think that faculty and experience should be put together, and that I have both of them and should be using them this minute to write an article for K., the famous compiler of philosophical mouthings and professorial snacks of wisdom and snippets of advice and so on, and here I sit trying to tell K. how miserable I really am because I am old and rapidly spoiling (i.e., rotting away in a puddle of blood and tears—"no sweat," as you might say), but instead my eyes keep going out the window to watch the sun on the dancing leaves. My poor old body is out there too. The grass looks beautiful, a sudden tender green after last night's little rain, and the red lava stones look redder than usual, and the vines have a new fuzz of green on them. In other words I feel like spring.

You say that in what I wrote about Henry Volkening there was no war between telling the truth and expressing affection. Of course there was not. Why should there be? I feel the same way about you. I think right now that you are peevish and grumpy about being old, and I don't want you to be because I love you. But the truth is that you *are* grumpy this minute. Of course you have a right to be, very simply because your age gives you that privilege. I honestly feel, though, that you are grumpy because you are frightened, and I am very impatient about that because by now you should know better. You've had a whole lifetime to face the fact that you too will be old and sad and aching, and now that you are old you are suddenly angry at being so.

Unfortunately, most people who have the rare experience of being your age and mine are exactly the same as you. They deliberately choose to close their eyes until it happens, and then they are peeved as hell that it has happened. It may be because they are just plain stupid, either deliberately or by nature. I would not call you stupid by nature certainly, but I think you are dumb (i.e., stupid) to feel so astonished that you, *too,* actually must go through the indignity of having a cataract removed from *your* eye. It's the first cataract removed ever from any eye, of course (empathy?), and you have the gall to ask me if I've ever had an eye or cataract operation. Hell, man, I've had two! And the only reason I'm not having it done at least once more is that I see no reason at all to risk bothering.

You say, "Old age is fascinating"—and I see your curled lip and the fake jauntiness and the hidden mockery cum bravery etc., etc., and I refuse to reply. You go on that something peculiar happens every minute, and I agree completely with you. It sure as hell does happen every minute, and I look out the window and the leaves are getting dancier than ever and suddenly I feel like shooting my wheelchair across the tiles, and then your letter floats onto the tile floor and I can't even pick it up and I start to titter and so does my helpless friend who is typing for me, and altogether I feel quite silly and giddy and happy, and I am not at all peeved at you, poor man.

—*Glen Ellen, California, 1989*

66

Query

Perhaps the best thing about finding oneself old is trying not to be as dull and boring as all one's peers. Taking a look around can be depressing, but learning from what one sees is often very helpful in holding off the suppressed yawns that accompany almost any public appearance of an old person among potential grandchildren.

It's painful—devastating—to catch a badly suppressed look of complete resigned ennui on a young face, over a glass or teacup. It may be even worse to notice, suddenly, that one's amusing anecdote about Great-Aunt Mary's clumsy curtsy to Queen Victoria has already been told several times to the same dutiful young descendant.

Why is it that most people over fifty forget that they once hated their parents, and that they too tried to put a cow in the campanile or pin huge butterflies to the hands of the town clock? Why do people kicking sixty or seventy in the ass forget to watch for the glazed grin, that nodding courtesy, that they once showed to their own almost unbearably boring grandparents?

Have the scales grown willy-nilly over our spiritual eyes, the money become cotton in our ears? Or do we old people *want* to feel ignored, neglected, scorned, sad?

—Glen Ellen, California, mid-1980s

67

Medication

This is very difficult for me but it is something I am thinking about a great deal. I'll try to say it while I can.

It seems very ironic to me that at this point in my life, which I have spent consciously and unconsciously in talking to myself, I find it very hard to express my thoughts. I have always boasted, or at least I have said what seemed very true to me, that I am not a writer. I have written nothing but what I was speaking or saying to myself, and over the years I have developed a certain skill at this trick. I think always in phrases and sentences and paragraphs and even chapters. They are all a conversation with myself, in the true sense of the word *conversation*.

I am sometimes very dull, but I go right on talking, and at times I'm very witty or even funny, so that I find it hard not to laugh aloud, and still my mind goes on. But now after almost eighty years, during which I've practiced this strange art of private conversation and put it down in stories and essays and suchlike, I am increasingly incapable of conversing in any form. I can no longer write by hand, nor by machine, and mostly I am without a voice. In the morning I am better and can even say a few words that can be heard by a few other people, but they are without real meaning. Lately, I find that I tend to listen more to radio than I usually do to television. With the latter, I close my eyes mostly. They seem to tire easily and I never read a word anymore. Sometimes late at night from about three in the morning they are bright, and I watch whatever is on TV. I find that my powers are diminishing fast, partly because I'm not using them, but mostly because I tire easily. And lately, I must make this effort to speak clearly . . .

I feel I should continue to write this but will put it off until Marsha comes again, and then I will start it fresh and perhaps I will speak more clearly about this strange condition. I think of it a lot and I want to leave some record for Norah and Marsha and Pat. My medication makes my mouth very dry, which complicates the problem.

That's all for now.

—Glen Ellen, California, 1991

68

Notes on the Craft, Skill, Science, or Art of Missing

There is a commercial on, about a car called the Charger. A light-voiced man mimics an old-time vaudevillian. His timing is perfect, his mimicry impeccable. I prepare a salad or wash panty-hose or something on that level, the sound going on, and suddenly at a certain combination of rhythm–timing–voice play I am engulfed by a wrenching sense of missing June.

She and I never listened to this sort of music. There was always some going on, but she liked a schmaltzier beat than I did. When I stayed at her house I listened to it and enjoyed it. She liked big orchestras and a certain amount of uncluttered lilt.

When I lived for several years at my growing-up place, to help my widowed father a little and give my two small girls a good dignified man to know, June came as often as she could to stay for a couple of days with us. She and Father hit it off. We all did, and it was always fine.

He was deaf, though, and early in the mornings (he had breakfast and an hour of dictation before he got to his office at nine) we would be in the old kitchen. June would sit on a high stool, and I would be organizing his tray, coffee and all that, and a good meal for the kids and on weekdays their lunches, and we would listen to Fats Waller and Jelly Roll Morton.

I had the run Jelly Roll did with Lomax for the Library of Congress or wherever it was. (I still have it, but seldom listen to it now. I've heard it, thank God.) June would start out with a small cup of fresh coffee and then have a small glass of half water and half bourbon, while I moved around, my back mostly to her, and readied the other morning niceties, and changed records on the "box" I kept in the kitchen, as essential to me as the stove-freezer-refrigerator-toaster-ice crusher—all at the command of a person who hates gadgets.

Behind me I would know that June sat cross-legged on top of the stool, glass nearby, her eyes now and then filled with glad tears at a special word or sound from the old records. She was far from that kitchen, in a world nobody but she could ever fathom, and the trip there had some pain in it but she was willing to share it with her other selves and with me in those mornings when Rex, my father and our mutual friend, could snooze a bit later . . .

Now and then I would prance around a bit, at the stove or icebox, and she would chuckle, because we were both high on the music that pounded out. Long before in our separate lives we had heard it in different places, but those weekend mornings with light coming through the walnut tree by the kitchen windows at the Ranch, a good hour before my father and the little girls woke up, were a shared experience that is valuable enough to miss, in the highest sense of that word.

Tonight when I listen to that high affected voice, reminiscent of the old Orpheum circuit rather than what June and I listened to on early Sundays, the timing is part of other better jazzmen, and abruptly I am wracked by a sense of missing. I miss June. I miss being able to listen to the same music. Why did she dodge the trap before I did?

I feel puzzled about all of this. Why do I not miss my sister Anne at all? Now and then I have poignant regrets about how I failed her sometimes in her life, and how confused she was (to my mind), and how I tried with fairly complete nonsuccess to help her through financial-legal-emotional fiascoes. But I do not miss her. I am glad she has solved her own secret problems, although to do it she had to die a dog's death.

She introduced me to June, whom I miss more strongly.

I also miss one dog and one cat. The dog was registered as P'ing Cho Fung, but in the days when Butch did not necessarily mean a dyke haircut, I named him that defiantly, against his titles, and that he was. He was a highly dignified Pekingese dog. Now and then his spirit approaches my subconscious, and I feel that he is beside me, perhaps touching my hand subtly with his nose like a cool rose petal. And the cat, Blackberry, was ruler of the current roost, and by now is part of a hierarchy of the three great cats I have been privileged to harbor among countless lesser pensioners. He was a formidable friend.

There are other animals I miss almost physically, at times, as much as the two-legged ones like June. But here I must pull myself up, as I would a young pony, to ask what I mean by the word *miss*.

I can try to say that Missing is partly physical. There is a strong pull back to the warm kitchen with Jelly Roll and the friend cross-legged on the high stool, the friend gone now; to the princely little dog, also gone now. It is a wrench that is almost orgiastic, if one permits it to be, and it is always ready to pounce at unexpected moments, as when a canny-silly commercial comes over the radio.

Missing is also a more inward condition. It is something that must be accepted as part of any thinking existence, and made use of. It is a force. The special flavor of true Missing should be channeled. It is very strong. And I like to hope that the stronger the person is who misses something or someone, the stronger the force will be.

It continues to puzzle me that I miss June more than I miss my sister. It comes down to the fact, perhaps, that I am glad one died and sorry the other did. But I am not glad that Butch died. I am not glad that Blackberry did, either.

What is left is a vulnerable spot in my acceptance of vulnerability. These and many other people, like lovers and husbands and even friends, have slid off the scales. They seem, now and then for unknown reasons, to stand there stark and grabbing, in front of us. They want us. We say, No, not now. But the statement is a painful one.

That is why it hurts me when that silly commercial comes on, about some car named Charger that is selling for less than cost. The rhythm and timing—exquisite. The inexplicable anguish, fleeting but poignant to the point of true pain, of missing June, the little dog, perhaps a dozen other true beings, brought out by that shoddy takeoff: why should I submit to it? And why should it make me wonder why I loved them and not some other people?

—*Glen Ellen, California, mid-1980s*

About the Author

M. F. K. Fisher was born in Albion, Michigan, in 1908 and spent most of her childhood in Whittier, California. During ensuing years she lived in Dijon, Vevey, Aix-en-Provence, and southern California before moving to the northern California wine country in 1954. She authored over sixteen volumes of essays and reminiscences, including *The Art of Eating, Two Towns in Provence, Among Friends,* and a widely admired translation of Brillat-Savarin's *The Physiology of Taste.* Fisher's two earlier volumes of reminiscences, *To Begin Again* and *Stay Me, Oh Comfort Me,* were published by Pantheon, respectively, in 1992 and 1993. For the last twenty years of her life she lived in a house built for her in Glen Ellen, California. She died at Last House on June 22, 1992.